HMH Florida Science

Grade 3

This Write-In Book belongs to

_____

Teacher/Room

_____

The loggerhead sea turtle makes its nests along the coasts of Florida. Adult turtles weigh an average of 250 pounds!

Houghton Mifflin Harcourt

Consulting Authors

Michael A. DiSpezio
Global Educator
North Falmouth, Massachusetts

Marjorie Frank
*Science Writer and Content-Area Reading
   Specialist*
Brooklyn, New York

Michael R. Heithaus, Ph.D.
*Dean, College of Arts, Sciences & Education
Professor, Department of Biological Sciences*
Florida International University
Miami, Florida

Houghton Mifflin Harcourt

Cover: ©Khoroshunova Olga Underwater/Alamy

ISBN   978-1-328-79358-4

15   1468   28 27 26 25 24 23
4500869217   CDEFG

Contents

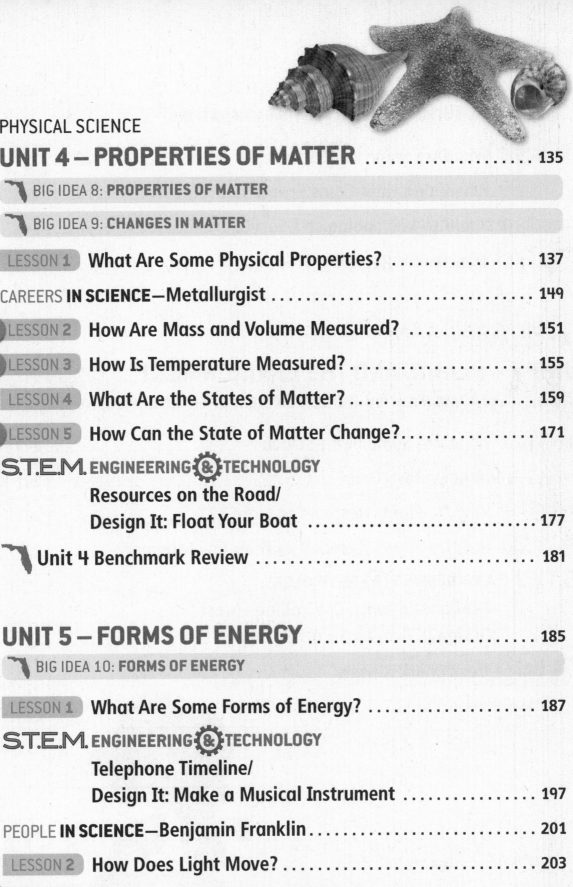

LIFE SCIENCE

UNIT 8 – CLASSIFYING PLANTS AND ANIMALS 287

UNIT 9 – LIVING THINGS CHANGE 331

Safety in Science

Doing investigations in science can be fun, but you need to be sure you do them safely. Here are some rules to follow.

1. Think ahead.

Study the steps of the investigation so you know what to expect. If you have any questions, ask your teacher. Be sure you understand any caution statements or safety reminders.

2. Be neat.

Keep your work area clean. If you have long hair, pull it back so it doesn't get in the way. Roll or push up long sleeves to keep them away from your experiment.

3. Oops!

If you spill or break something, or if you get cut, tell your teacher right away.

4. Watch your eyes.

Wear safety goggles anytime you are directed to do so. If you get anything in your eyes, tell your teacher right away.

5. Yuck!

Never eat or drink anything during a science activity.

6. Don't get shocked.

Be especially careful if an electric appliance is used. Be sure that electrical cords are in a safe place where you can't trip over them. Never pull a plug out of an outlet by pulling on the cord.

7. Keep it clean.

Always clean up when you have finished. Put everything away and wipe your work area. Wash your hands.

Investigating Questions

A scientist uses binoculars to see animals that are far away.

FLORIDA **BIG IDEA 1**

The Practice of Science

FLORIDA **BIG IDEA 3**

The Role of Theories, Laws, Hypotheses, and Models

I Wonder Why

South Florida is home to many animals, such as sea turtles. How do scientists help animals survive? *Turn the page to find out.*

Here's Why

Scientists in Florida work on land and water! They use tools such as tags, cameras, notes, and maps to help animals survive.

Essential Questions and Florida Benchmarks

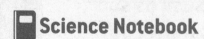

Science Notebook

Before you begin each lesson, write your thoughts about the Essential Question.

SC.3.N.1.1 Raise questions about the natural world . . . SC.3.N.1.6 Infer based on observation. SC.3.N.3.1 Recognize that words in science can have different or more specific meanings than their use in everyday language; for example, energy, cell, heat/cold, and evidence. SC.3.N.3.2 Recognize that scientists use models . . . SC.3.N.3.3 Recognize that all models are approximations of natural phenomena . . .

LESSON 1

ESSENTIAL **QUESTION**

How Do Scientists Investigate Questions?

Engage Your Brain

Find the answer to the following question in this lesson and record it here.

How is this student acting like a scientist?

_____

_____

_____

ACTIVE **READING**

Lesson Vocabulary
List each term. As you learn about each, make notes in the Interactive Glossary.

_____   _____

_____   _____

_____

_____

Use Headings
Active readers preview, or read, the headings first. Headings give the reader an idea of what the reading is about. Reading with a purpose helps active readers understand what they are reading.

3

What Is Science?

Science is about Earth and everything beyond it. What does a scientist look like? To find out, take a look in the mirror!

ACTIVE **READING** As you read these two pages, underline the main idea.

Why do volcanoes erupt?

Look for a Question

How does a butterfly use its six legs? What does the shape of a cloud tell about the weather? It's never too soon to start asking questions! Write your own question below.

_____

_____

Science is a way of looking at the world and thinking about it. When you think like a scientist, you ask questions about the world around you. You try to answer your questions by doing investigations.

Some investigations are simple, such as watching animals play. Other investigations take planning. You need to gather and set up materials. Then you write down what happens.

You can think like a scientist on your own or in a group. Sharing what you learn is part of the fun. So get started!

Why does a compass point north?

What do stars look like through a telescope?

What Do You See?

So you want to think like a scientist? Let's get started. Try making some observations and inferences!

ACTIVE **READING** As you read these two pages, find and underline the definition of *observe*.

Look at the pictures on this page. What do you see? When you use your senses to notice details, you **observe**.

Things you observe can start you thinking. Look at the picture of the small sailboat. You see that it has more than one sail. Now look more closely. The sails are different shapes and sizes.

You might infer that the shape or size of the sails affects how the boat moves. When you **infer**, you offer an explanation of what you observed. You might infer that each sail helps the boat move in a different way.

Make an observation about this boat.

_____

_____

_____

Make an observation about this ship.

_____

_____

CONTAINER SHIP

Make an observation about this boat.

_____

_____

623   U. S. COAST GUARD

Write an inference based on this observation: "I can see the wind blowing this sail."

_____

_____

Getting Answers!

People ask questions all day long. But not all questions are science questions. Science questions can be answered in many ways.

ACTIVE **READING** As you read these two pages, circle a common, everyday word that has a different meaning in science.

Exploring

Some science questions can be answered by exploring. Say you see a leaf float by on the water. You wonder what else can float on water. You find an eraser in your pocket. You **predict,** or use what you know to tell if it will sink or float. When you know which items float and which don't, you can **classify,** or group, them.

Predict

Think about each item pictured. Then circle the ones you predict will float. Mark an X on those you predict will sink.

Investigating

You might think of an investigation as looking for clues. In science, an **investigation** is a planned way of finding answers to questions. When you do an investigation, you might ask a cause-and-effect question, "Does the amount of weight in a boat affect whether it floats or sinks?" Because you don't want to use a real boat, you can **make and use models.** A raft made of sticks is not exactly like a real boat, but it can be used to learn about them.

Investigating Answers

There are many steps a scientist may take during an investigation. Some do all five described here.

ACTIVE READING As you read these two pages, number the sentences that describe Onisha's experiment to match the numbered steps in the circles.

1 Ask a Question

What causes things to change? This is the kind of question you can answer with an investigation.

2 Hypothesize

A **hypothesis** is a statement that could answer your question. You must be able to test a hypothesis.

3 Predict and Plan an Investigation

Predict what you will observe if your hypothesis is correct. **Identify the variable** to test, and keep other variables the same.

What Onisha Did ...

Onisha thought about rafts floating down a river. She asked a question, "Does the size of a raft affect the amount of weight it can carry?"

Onisha **hypothesized** that a bigger raft can carry more weight. Then she predicted, "I should be able to add more weight to a bigger raft than to a smaller raft." Onisha planned an investigation called an experiment. Outside of science, experimenting means trying something new, such as a new recipe. In science, an **experiment** is a test done to gather evidence. The evidence might support the hypothesis, or it might not. In her experiment, Onisha built three model rafts that differed only in their number of planks. She carefully put one penny at a time onto each raft until it sank. She recorded her results and drew a conclusion.

Variable

The factor that is changed in an experiment is called a **variable**. It's important to change only one variable at a time.

Draw Conclusions

Analyze your results, and **draw a conclusion.** Ask yourself, "Do the results support my hypothesis?" Share your conclusion with others.

4 Experiment

Now do the experiment to test your hypothesis.

5

▶ What was the variable in Onisha's experiment?

_____

_____

Write words from the lesson that match the pictures.

1. _____

2. _____

The small plane will fly farther.

3. _____

4. _____

Use what you learned from the lesson to fill in the sequence below.

observe ➡ 5. _____

6. _____ ➡ 7. _____

Brain Check

Name _____

Vocabulary Review

1 Draw a line from each term to its definition or description.

1. experiment*

2. infer*

3. questions

4. investigation*

5. variable*

6. hypothesis*

7. predict*

8. model

9. observe*

10. conclusion

A. You do this when you make a conclusion after observing.

B. the one factor you can change in an experiment

C. to make a guess based on what you know or think

D. something that is like the real thing – but not exactly

E. a statement that will answer a question you want to investigate

F. Scientists plan and carry one out to answer their questions

G. Scientists ask these about the world around them.

H. You do this when you use your five senses.

I. an investigation in which you use variables

J. You draw this at the end of an investigation.

*Key Lesson Vocabulary

Apply Concepts

2 This bridge is over the Mississippi River. List materials you could use to make a model of it.

_____

_____

3 Greyson wants to know what plants need in order to survive. He places one plant in a window. He places another plant in a dark closet. What is the variable he is testing?

_____

4 Jared looks carefully at a young turtle in his hand. Label each of his statements *observation* or *inference*.

Its front legs are longer than its back legs. _____

It has sharp toenails. _____

It uses its toenails to dig. _____

It can see me. _____

Its shell feels cool and dry against my hand. _____

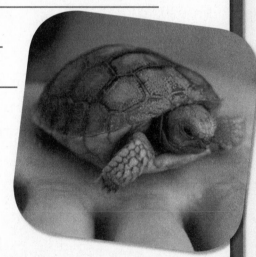

Take It Home! See *ScienceSaurus*® for more information about questions.

SC.3.N.1.3 Keep records as appropriate, such as pictorial, written, or simple charts and graphs, of investigations conducted. SC.3.N.1.6 Infer based on observation. SC.3.N.3.2 Recognize that scientists use models to help understand and explain how things work. SC.3.N.3.3 Recognize that all models are approximations of natural phenomena; as such, they do not perfectly account for all observations.

INQUIRY
LESSON 2

Name _____

ESSENTIAL QUESTION

How Can You Use a Model?

EXPLORE

Have you ever wondered why a plane can fly? Since a real plane is too big for you to investigate, a model is the next best thing.

Before You Begin—Preview the Steps

(1) Make your model airplane.

(2) CAUTION: Wear goggles. Fly your airplane in a safe place. Use the meterstick to measure how far it flies each time.

(3) Write a hypothesis about what changes would make the plane go farther.

(4) Test your hypothesis by changing your plane and measuring the distance it flies.

Set a Purpose

What is the question you will try to answer with this investigation?

_____

_____

_____

State Your Hypothesis

Write your hypothesis, or testable statement.

_____

_____

_____

_____

Think About the Procedure

What is the variable you plan to test?

_____

_____

How will you know whether the variable you changed worked?

_____

_____

_____

_____

Name _____

Record Your Data

Fill in the chart to record how far the plane flew each time you changed its design.

Change Made to the Model	Distance It Flew

Draw Conclusions

How is your model alike and different from a real airplane?

_____

_____

_____

_____

Claims • Evidence • Reasoning

1. Interpret your data. Write a claim about which changes to your model worked best.

_____

_____

2. Cite evidence from the activity that supports your claim and explain why the evidence supports the claim.

_____

_____

_____

Claims • Evidence • Reasoning (continued)

3. Write a claim about whether your hypothesis was supported by your results. Cite evidence that supports your claim and explain why it supports the claim.

_____

_____

_____

_____

4. What did you learn about real airplanes from using a model?

_____

_____

_____

5. What can't you learn about real airplanes by using a paper airplane? Explain your reasoning.

_____

_____

_____

_____

6. Think of another question you would like to answer about airplane models.

_____

_____

_____

SC.3.N.1.1 Raise questions about the natural world... **SC.3.N.1.2** Compare the observations made by different groups using the same tools and seek reasons to explain the differences across groups. **SC.3.N.1.3** Keep records as appropriate, such as pictorial, written, or simple charts and graphs . . .

ESSENTIAL **QUESTION**

How Do Scientists Use Tools?

Engage Your Brain

A hand lens can make a bug look bigger.

What other tools make objects look bigger?

_____

_____

📖 ACTIVE **READING**

Lesson Vocabulary
List each term. As you learn about each one, make notes in the Interactive Glossary.

_____

_____

_____

Compare and Contrast
Ideas in parts of this lesson explain comparisons and contrasts—they tell how things are alike and different. Active readers focus on comparisons and contrasts when they ask questions such as, How are measuring tools alike and different?

Make It Clear!

Scientists use tools to give them super-vision! Some tools that do this include hand lenses and microscopes.

ACTIVE **READING** As you read these two pages, circle words or phrases that signal when things are alike and different.

Light microscopes let you see tiny objects by using a light source and lenses or mirrors inside the microscope.

A magnifying box has a lens in its lid.

A hand lens has one lens with a handle.

Use forceps to pick up tiny objects to view with magnifiers.

Use a dropper to move small amounts of liquids for viewing.

Close, Closer, Closest!

Magnifying tools make objects look larger. Hold a hand lens close to one eye. Then move the hand lens closer to the object until it looks large and sharp. A magnifying box is like a hand lens in that it also has one lens. You can put things that are hard to hold, such as a bug, in it.

A **microscope** magnifies objects that are too tiny to be seen with the eye alone. Its power is much greater than that of a hand lens or magnifying box. Most microscopes have two or more lenses that work together.

▶ Draw a picture of how something you see might look if it was magnified.

Pond water as seen with just your eyes.

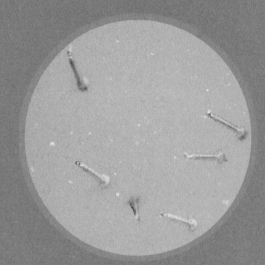

Pond water as seen through a hand lens.

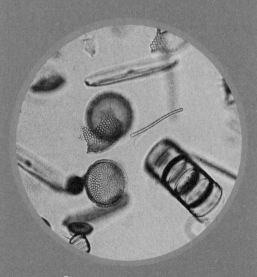

Pond water as seen through a microscope.

21

Measure It!

Measuring uses numbers to describe the world around you. There are several ways to measure and more than one tool or unit for each way.

ACTIVE **READING** As you read the next page, circle the main idea.

A balance has a pan on either side. Put the object you want to measure on one pan and add masses to the other pan until they are balanced. The basic unit of mass is the gram.

The units on measuring tapes can be centimeters and meters or inches and feet.

ruler

A graduated cylinder has units of volume marked on its side.

Length, Mass, and Volume

Every tool has its purpose! You can **measure** length with rulers and tape measures. Mass is the amount of matter in an object. It is measured with a pan balance. Volume is the amount of space a solid, liquid, or gas takes up.

The volume of a liquid can be measured with a **graduated cylinder** or a measuring cup or spoon. You can also use these tools to find the volume of solids that can be poured, such as sugar or salt. You **use numbers** to report measurements and **compare** objects. You can also **order** things using measurements. You can put pencils in order from shortest to longest.

Measuring cups and spoons are used because the amount of each ingredient is very important.

DO THE MATH

Subtract Units

Use a metric ruler to measure the parts of the frog.

1. How many centimeters is the frog's longest front leg?

   _____

2. How many centimeters is the frog's longest back leg?

   _____

3. Now find the difference.

   _____

4. Compare your measurements to those of other students.

   _____

   _____

Time and Temperature

How long did that earthquake shake? Which freezes faster, hot water or cold water? Scientists need tools to answer these questions!

Time

When you count the steady drip of a leaky faucet, you are thinking about time. You can **use time and space relationships.** Clocks and stopwatches are tools that measure time. The base unit of time is the second. One minute is equal to 60 seconds. One hour is equal to 60 minutes.

What if frogs held swim races across a pond? Here two frogs are racing.

START!

Temperature

When you say that ovens are hot or freezers are cold, you are thinking about **temperature**. A thermometer is the tool used to measure temperature. The base units of temperature are called degrees, but all degrees are not the same.

Scientists usually measure temperature in degrees Celsius. Most people around the world use Celsius, too. In the United States, however, degrees Fahrenheit are used to report the weather, body temperature, and in cooking.

▶ The first frog finished the race in 19 seconds. The second frog finished the race in 47 seconds. How much more quickly did the winning frog finish the race?

_____

_____

_____

How Do You Care for Tropical Fish?

To care for tropical fish, you have to think like a scientist and use science tools.

Close Encounters

A public aquarium [uh•KWAIR•ee•uhm] is the place to see sharks and tropical fish. That's where many people get excited about keeping tropical fish at home. The word *aquarium* is used for both the big place you visit and the small tank in your home. Caring for both takes similar skills: observing, inferring, measuring, and recording data.

Does moving your aquarium in front of the window change the water's temperature?

What is the volume of water in your aquarium?

Keep Good Records

Keeping good records is important, whether you're recording data in your science notebook or making entries in your aquarium log. In your log, record the temperature every time you check it. Write the time you feed the fish and the volume of food you give them. Making correct measurements is part of being a good scientist.

Water test kits identify materials in the water.

Taking care of fish means checking the temperature.

Cause and Effect

Every change in an aquarium has a cause. Sometimes fish in an aquarium might become sick. Think of two things that might cause the fish to get sick.

_____

_____

_____

Sum It Up »

The idea web below summarizes this lesson. Complete the web.

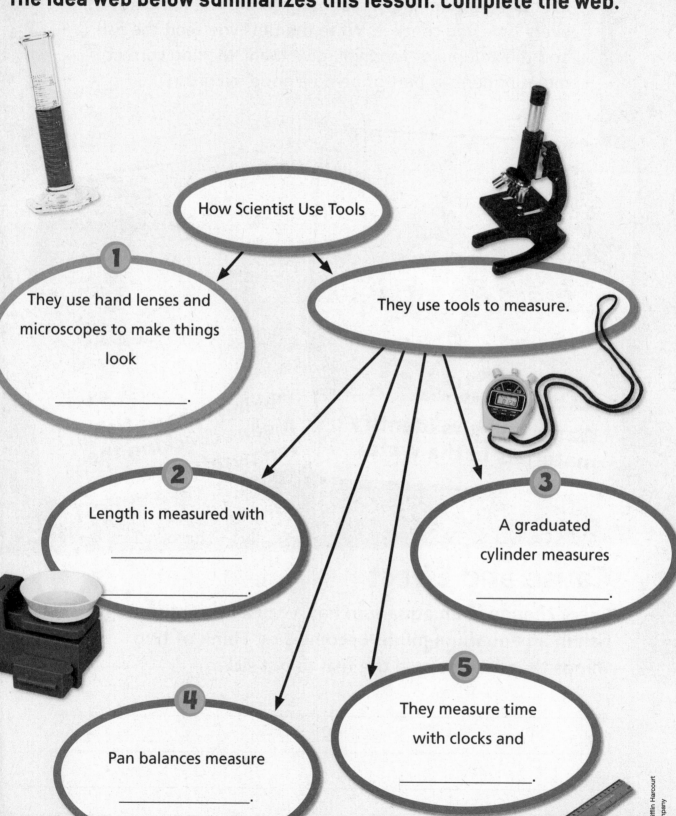

How Scientist Use Tools

1 They use hand lenses and microscopes to make things look

_____.

They use tools to measure.

2 Length is measured with

_____

_____.

3 A graduated cylinder measures

_____.

4 Pan balances measure

_____.

5 They measure time with clocks and

_____.

Name _____

Vocabulary Review

1 Use the clues to fill in the missing letters of the words.

1. p _ _ _ _ _ a n _ _   a tool used to measure mass

2. C _ _ _ _ u _   a temperature scale used by scientists

3. _ _ _ _ e p _   a tool used to pick up tiny objects

4. _ _ _ _ _ a t _ _ _ _ l _ _ _ _ r   a tool used to measure volume

5. _ _ n _ _ _ _ s   a tool you hold against your eye to make objects look bigger

6. _ _ _ _ e _ a _ _ _ _   how hot or cold something is

7. _ _ _ _ m o m _ _ _ _   a tool used to measure temperature

8. t _ _ _   something you measure with a stopwatch

9. _ _ _ u m _   how much space something takes up

Apply Concepts

In 2–5, tell which tool(s) you would use and how you would use them.

 thermometer

measuring spoons

 measuring tape

ruler

magnifying box

2 Find out how long your dog is from nose to tail.

_____

_____

_____

3 Decide if you need to wear a sweatshirt outdoors.

_____

_____

4 Make a bubble bath that has just the right amount of bubbles and is not too hot or too cold.

_____

_____

_____

_____

5 Examine a ladybug and count its legs without hurting it.

_____

_____

_____

SC.3.N.1.1 Raise questions about the natural world, investigate . . . and generate appropriate explanations . . . SC.3.N.1.2 Compare the observations made by different groups . . . SC.3.N.1.3 Keep records . . . of investigations conducted. SC.3.N.1.4 Recognize the importance of communication . . . SC.3.N.1.7 Explain that empirical evidence is information . . . used to help validate explanations of natural phenomena.

INQUIRY LESSON 4

Name _____

ESSENTIAL QUESTION

How Can You Measure Length?

Materials

- meterstick
- metric ruler
- string
- metric measuring tape
- objects from tear-out sheet

EXPLORE

There are many tools and units for measuring length or distance. In this activity, you will explore which tools and units to use in different situations.

Before You Begin—Preview the Steps

1. Choose a tool and unit to measure the longest distance across your classroom. Then measure it.

2. Now choose another tool and unit and measure the same distance across the classroom.

3. Choose a tool and unit to measure each object on your sheet. Then measure each item.

4. Compare your choices and measurements with other students. Discuss the differences.

Set a Purpose

What will you be able to do at the end of this investigation?

_____

_____

_____

Think About the Procedure

What will you think about when choosing the measurement tool for each item?

_____

_____

_____

_____

How will you choose the units that are best for each item?

_____

_____

_____

_____

Name _____

Record Your Data

In the space below, make a table in which you
record your measurements.

Draw Conclusions

How does choosing the best tool make measuring length easier?

_____

_____

_____

Claims • Evidence • Reasoning

1. Think about the investigation. Write a claim about how the units you use to
   measure affect the quality of a measurement.

   _____

   _____

2. Cite evidence and reasons based on activity that support your claim and explain
   why the evidence and reasons support the claim.

   _____

   _____

   _____

Claims • Evidence • Reasoning (continued)

3. Did groups who used the same tools as your group get the same results as you? Explain why or why not.

_____

_____

_____

4. Why was it important to communicate your results with other groups? Explain your reasoning.

_____

_____

_____

5. When would someone want to use millimeters to find out who throws a ball the farthest? When would using millimeters not be a good choice? Explain your reasoning. (1,000 mm = 1 m)

_____

_____

_____

_____

6. Think of another question you would like to ask about measuring.

_____

_____

Name _____

Materials
Which tools should you use?

Garter snake

Hemlock tree cone

Ladybug beetle

Bird's feather

SC.3.N.1.1 Raise questions about the natural world . . . SC.3.N.1.2 Compare the observations made by different groups . . . SC.3.N.1.3 Keep records as appropriate . . . SC.3.N.1.4 Recognize the importance of communication . . . SC.3.N.1.5 Recognize that scientists question, discuss, and check each others' evidence and explanations. SC.3.N.1.7 Explain that empirical evidence...is used to help validate explanations . . .

LESSON 5

ESSENTIAL QUESTION

How Do Scientists Record Data?

 Engage Your Brain

People sometimes make statues out of blocks. If you could count how many blocks of each color there are, how would you record this information?

_____

_____

_____

_____

ACTIVE READING

Lesson Vocabulary
List each term. As you learn about each one, make notes in the Interactive Glossary.

_____   _____

_____   _____

Main Ideas
The main idea of a section is the most important idea. The main idea may be stated in the first sentence, or it may be stated elsewhere. Active readers look for main ideas by asking themselves, What is this section mostly about?

Show Me the Evidence

Scientists use observations to answer their questions. You can do this, too!

ACTIVE **READING** As you read these two pages, find and underline the definitions of *data* and *evidence*.

My data is my *evidence*. It shows that a raft with six planks floats twice as much weight as a raft with only three planks.

Onisha, how do you know that a bigger raft can float more weight than a smaller one?

- I put the pennies on the raft with three planks. It held fewer pennies than the other raft.

Each science observation is a piece of **data.** For example, the number of pennies on a raft is data.

Onisha finished her investigation and thought about what it meant. She studied her data. Scientists use data as **evidence** to decide whether a hypothesis is or is not supported. Either way, scientists learn valuable things.

Scientists ask other scientists a lot of questions. They compare data. They repeat the investigation to see if they get the same results. Scientists review and talk about the evidence. They agree and disagree while respecting each other's ideas.

Scientists might live too far away to meet face to face. What are three other ways they can share data and discuss evidence?

_____

_____

_____

_____

_____

_____

_____

Communicating Data

Scientists record and display data so others can understand it. There are many ways and many tools to do this.

How can I communicate my results?

Take a photograph.

You want to find how high different kinds of balls bounce. You test each ball 20 times. How will you record and display your measurements?

_____

_____

After you **gather data,** you can share, or **communicate,** it with others in different ways. How can you **record data?** To show how birds get seeds from a feeder, you can use a camera. To show how a cat cares for her kittens, write it in a journal.

Sometimes scientists use tables and graphs to help **interpret** and **display data.** A **data table** is a display that organizes data into rows and columns. A **bar graph** is used to compare data about different events or groups. Graphs make it easier to see patterns or relationships in data.

Make a bar graph or a data table.

Write in a journal.

You want to record the way the moon seems to change shape for four weeks. What would you use?

_____

_____

You want to describe the kinds of animals you observe living in a stream. Where would you record your observations?

_____

_____

Sum It Up »

Use information in the summary to complete the graphic organizer.

During investigations scientists record their observations, or data. When other scientists ask, "How do you know?", they explain how their data supports their answers. Observations can be shared in many ways. Data in the form of numbers can be shown in data tables and bar graphs. Data can also be shared as diagrams, photos, or in writing.

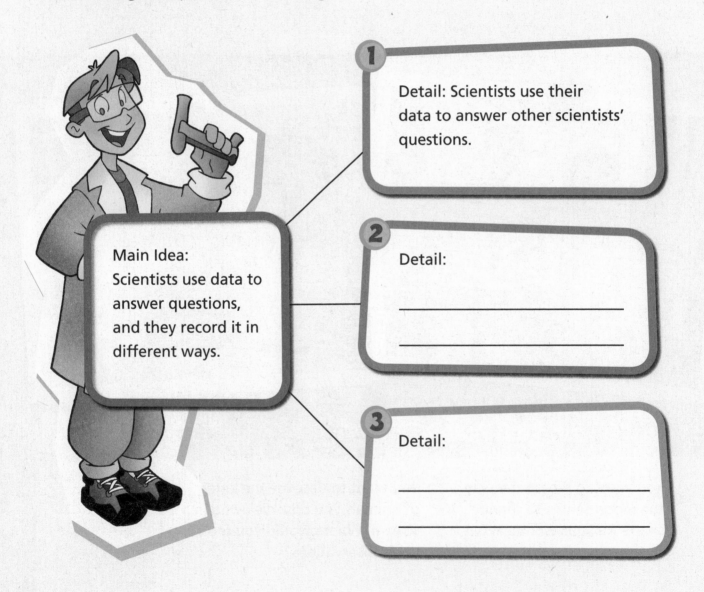

1 Detail: Scientists use their data to answer other scientists' questions.

Main Idea: Scientists use data to answer questions, and they record it in different ways.

2 Detail:

_____

_____

3 Detail:

_____

_____

Name _____

Vocabulary Review

Find the correct meaning and underline it.

1 Data

- a tool used to measure

- how hot or cold something is

- a piece of science information

2 Evidence

- a kind of graph

- how much space something takes up

- the facts that show if a hypothesis is correct

3 Data table

- a chart for recording numbers

- the number of planks on a raft

- a piece of furniture used by scientists

4 Bar graph

- a chart for recording numbers

- a graph in the shape of a circle

- a graph that shows how things compare

5 Communicate

- take a photograph

- share data with others

- collect and record data

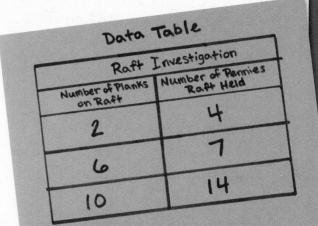

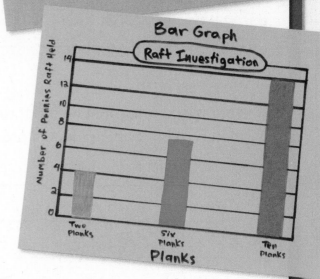

Apply Concepts

Read the story and answer questions 6–8.

One morning, your dad walks you and your sister to the school bus stop. When you get there, you wonder, "Has the bus come yet?"

6 What kinds of evidence would support the idea that the bus has not arrived yet?

_____

_____

7 What kinds of evidence would show that the bus had already come?

_____

_____

_____

8 Your friend brags that he can throw a baseball 100 meters. What evidence would prove this?

_____

_____

_____

_____

Take It Home! Share what you have learned about recording evidence with your family. With a family member, identify something you want to observe. Then decide how to record your data.

SC.3.N.1.1 Raise questions about the natural world . . . and generate appropriate explanations . . . SC.3.N.1.2 Compare the observations made by different groups . . . SC.3.N.1.3 Keep records as appropriate . . . SC.3.N.1.4 Recognize the importance of communication among scientists. SC.3.N.1.5 Recognize that scientists question, discuss, and check each others' evidence and explanations. SC.3.N.1.7 Explain that empirical evidence is . . . used to help validate explanations.

INQUIRY
LESSON 6

Name _____

ESSENTIAL QUESTION

How Do Your Results Compare?

Materials

3 plastic containers with lids

graduated cylinder

cold water

dropper

dishwashing liquid

metric ruler

EXPLORE

Bubbles are made when liquid soap is mixed with water. What happens when you add different amounts of soap?

Before You Begin—Preview the Steps

(1) Label the containers **A, B,** and **C.** Using the graduated cylinder to measure, pour 50 mL of water into each one.

(2) Using the dropper, put 5 drops of soap in container **A,** 10 drops in container **B,** and 15 drops in container **C.** Put the lids on.

(3) Shake container **A** five times. Measure the height of the bubbles in millimeters. Record the height. Repeat with the other containers.

(4) Rinse the containers and repeat Steps 1–3. Record your results. Compare your results with those of other groups.

Set a Purpose

What will you learn from this investigation?

_____

_____

_____

State Your Hypothesis

Tell how you think the height of bubbles in water relates to the amount of dishwashing liquid used. This is your hypothesis, or testable statement.

_____

_____

_____

Think About the Procedure

List the things you do that are the same each time.

_____

_____

_____

Identify the variable that you change each time.

_____

_____

_____

Name _____

Record Your Data

In the space below, make a table to record your measurements.

Draw Conclusions

What differences did you notice when you compared results with other groups?

_____

_____

_____

Claims • Evidence • Reasoning

1. Write a claim about whether your hypothesis was correct. Cite evidence that supports your claim and explain why it supports the claim.

_____

_____

_____

2. Why is it helpful to compare results with others?

_____

_____

_____

3. The bar graph shows the height of the column of bubbles produced by equal amounts of three brands of dishwashing liquid. Write a claim based on this data.

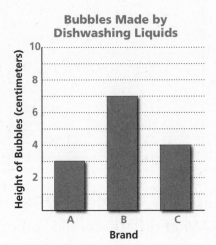

Bubbles Made by Dishwashing Liquids

_____

_____

4. Cite evidence from the graph that supports your claim and explain why the evidence supports the claim.

_____

_____

5. Think of other questions you would like to ask about bubbles.

_____

_____

SC.3.N.1.1 Raise questions about the natural world . . . **SC.3.N.1.3** Keep records as appropriate . . . **SC.3.N.1.7** Explain that empirical evidence...is used to help validate explanations . . .

CAREERS **IN SCIENCE**

1 A meteorologist is a person who studies weather.

2 Meteorologists use tools to measure temperature, wind speed, and air pressure.

6 Things You Should Know About
Meteorologists

3 Meteorologists use data they collect to forecast the weather.

4 Computers help meteorologists share weather data from around the world.

5 Keeping good records helps meteorologists see weather patterns.

6 Meteorologists' forecasts help people stay safe during bad weather.

Be a Meteorologist

Answer the questions below using the Weather Forecast bar graph.

1 What was the temperature on Thursday? _____

2 Which day was cloudy and rainy? _____

3 How much cooler was it on Tuesday than Thursday?
_____

4 Which day was partly cloudy? _____

5 Compare the temperatures on Tuesday and Friday. Which day had the higher temperature? _____

6 In the forecast below, which day has the highest temperature _____? The lowest? _____

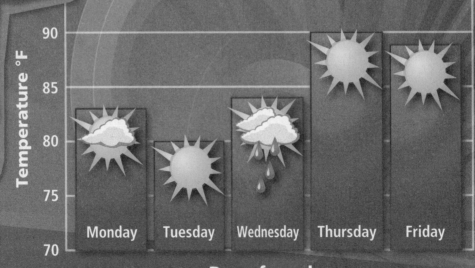

WEATHER FORECAST

Temperature °F

90
85
80
75
70

Monday Tuesday Wednesday Thursday Friday

Day of week

Name _____

Vocabulary Review

Use the terms in the box to complete the sentences.

bar graph
evidence
experiment
hypothesis
variable

1. You can share the results of an investigation with others

   by using a(n) _____.

2. An observation often leads to a testable question known as

   a(n) _____.

3. A planned study meant to answer a question is called

   a(n) _____.

4. It is very important to test only one _____, or
   thing that changes, at a time.

5. A claim should be supported by the _____.

Science Concepts

Fill in the letter of the choice that best answers the question.

6. Some shells have two parts. The animal
   can open the parts or close them tightly.
   The shell part in the picture
   is one that Yoshiko found.

   Which could be the other
   part of the shell Yoshiko found?

   Ⓐ    Ⓒ

   Ⓑ    Ⓓ

7. Omid did an experiment with radishes. He
   concluded that radishes grow best in full
   sunlight. He presents his experiment at a
   science fair. Why should Omid include his
   data with his presentation?

   Ⓕ The judges would have data to read.

   Ⓖ The judges would know he grew the
   plants.

   Ⓗ The judges would want to learn more
   about the topic.

   Ⓘ The judges could see if his data
   supported his conclusion.

8. A class is doing an experiment. The students want to know if tadpoles' health depends on the water they live in. They put the tadpoles into three tanks.

Tank	Type of water	Activity
A	clean tap water	Students will use treatments to keep the water clean.
B	clean tap water	Students will begin with clean water, but will not keep it clean.
C	clean tap water plus lots of dirt	Students will add a tablespoon of dirt every other day.

Which variable is being tested?

Ⓐ number of tanks

Ⓑ size of the tadpoles

Ⓒ amount of dirt in the water

Ⓓ amount of water in the tanks

9. Soon-Yi is using a model to investigate the parts of a plant in class. She cannot identify the part marked with an X.

Use the illustration to identify the part marked with an X.

X

Ⓕ bud   Ⓗ root

Ⓖ leaf   Ⓘ stem

10. Kia wants to know what types of trees grow the fastest. She looks at this table and sees she needs more information.

Age of tree (yr)	Height (m)
1	2
5	3
10	4
20	6

What information does she need?

Ⓐ the height of each tree

Ⓑ the age of each tree in months

Ⓒ the type of each tree that was measured

Ⓓ the date the trees were measured

11. Greyson observes a nest in a tree. What might Greyson infer about the nest?

Ⓕ The nest was made by a lizard.

Ⓖ The nest was made by a bird.

Ⓗ The nest does not have eggs in it.

Ⓘ The nest is made of grass.

Name _____

12. The bar graph below shows the number of students who have different types of pets.

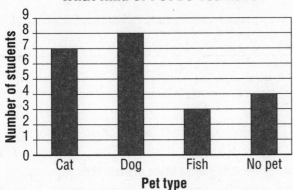

What Kind of Pet Do You Have?

Which statement is **best** supported by the data from the survey?

Ⓐ Some students do not have pets.

Ⓑ Most people do not like cats or dogs.

Ⓒ Most people like dogs more than they like cats.

Ⓓ Fish are easier to take care of than dogs or cats.

13. Mrs. Harris's class is doing an experiment to see if cut flowers stay fresh longer in warm water or cold water. Mrs. Harris created the table below.

	Roses	Daisies	Mums
Warm water			
Cold water			

What should students write in the different rows of the table?

Ⓕ the length of each stem

Ⓖ the size of each flower

Ⓗ the number of petals on each flower

Ⓘ the date each flower wilts

14. Three students observed the outside air temperature throughout the day. Their findings are below.

	8:15 a.m.	10:15 a.m.	12:15 p.m.	2:15 p.m.
Lucia	75 °F	78 °F	84 °F	89 °F
Ashok	75 °F	78 °F	85 °F	88 °F
Emily	75 °F	77 °F	84 °F	88 °F

The students recorded temperatures from their own thermometers in the same area each time. What could be a reason for the slight differences in the temperatures they recorded?

Ⓐ The students could not read the thermometers.

Ⓑ The students looked at the thermometers at different times.

Ⓒ One of the thermometers was broken so its readings were different.

Ⓓ Some of the readings were in between the marks so the students decided which mark was closest.

15. Why is it important to use scientific terms to describe clouds that you observe?

Ⓕ All clouds look the same.

Ⓖ Different cloud types are likely to appear at different times.

Ⓗ If you describe a cloud as an animal, people will not believe you.

Ⓘ People may have different ideas of "fluffy" or "thin," but the scientific terms are clearly defined.

Apply Inquiry and Review the Big Idea

Write the answers to these questions.

16. Make a claim about an object that would be easier to measure using a 25-ft tape measure than using a 12-inch ruler. Explain your reasoning.

_____

_____

_____

17. Eduardo fills six jars each with 400 mL of water. He places three of them outside in sunny spots. He places the other three outside in shady spots. He waits 4 hours. Then he measures how much water is left in each jar. He graphs the data. Make a claim about the rate at which water evaporates. Use evidence to support your claim and explain why it supports the claim.

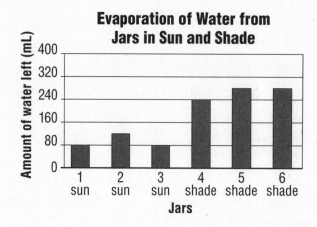

_____

_____

_____

_____

18. Mr. Martinez's class is testing objects that sink or float. They will use computer models. Identify an advantage and a disadvantage for using a computer model in this case.

_____

_____

_____

The Engineering Process

FLORIDA BIG IDEA 1

The Practice of Science

Ponce de Leon Inlet Lighthouse, south of Daytona

I Wonder Why

This building was built in 1883. How has the building process changed since then? Stayed the same? *Turn the page to find out.*

Here's Why

In 1883, tools were less complex than they are today, and they were not electric. But today's builders still have to draw plans, choose materials, and make sure the building is safe to use.

Essential Questions

Science Notebook

Before you begin each lesson, write your thoughts about the Essential Question.

SC.3.N.1.1 Raise questions about the natural world, investigate them individually and in teams through free exploration and systematic investigations, and generate appropriate explanations based on those explorations.
SC.3.N.1.7 Explain that empirical evidence is information, such as observations or measurements, that is used to help validate explanations of natural phenomena.

ESSENTIAL **QUESTION**

How Do Engineers Use the Design Process?

Engage Your Brain

Designs solve problems. What problem does the bridge solve?

_____

_____

📖 ACTIVE **READING**

Lesson Vocabulary
List the term. As you learn about it, make notes in the Interactive Glossary.

_____

Problem-Solution
Ideas in this lesson may be connected by a problem-solution relationship. Active readers mark a problem with a *P* to help them stay focused on the way information is organized. When solutions are described, active readers mark each solution with an *S*.

The Design Process

DESIGN PROCESS STEPS
1 Find a Problem
2 Plan & Build
3 Test & Improve
4 Redesign
5 Communicate

To get to school, you may have ridden your bike or taken the bus. These are two different ways of getting to school, but they have something in common.

ACTIVE **READING** As you read this page, circle the five steps of the design process and number each step.

Both of the methods of transportation above were developed by someone who used the design process. The **design process** is the process engineers follow to solve problems. It is a multistep process that includes finding a problem, planning and building, testing and improving, redesigning, and communicating results.

The William H. Natcher Bridge makes crossing the Ohio River easy and fast!

An engineer used the design process to design the supports for this bridge.

The design process can help people solve problems or design creative solutions. Look at the picture of the Ohio River between Rockport, Indiana, and Owensboro, Kentucky. In the past, only one bridge connected these cities. Over time, the bridge got very crowded. In this lesson, you'll see how the design process was used to design a solution to this problem.

How Do Inventions Help You?

Think of an invention that has made your life easier. What problem did it solve? How do you think the inventor used the design process to find the solution?

_____

_____

_____

_____

_____

Finding
a Problem

The design process starts with finding a problem. An engineer can't design a solution without first knowing what the problem is!

ACTIVE **READING** As you read these two pages, put brackets [ ] around sentences that describe the problem, and write *P* in front of the brackets. Put brackets around sentences that describe the steps toward a solution, and write *S* in front of the brackets.

A team of scientists and engineers worked together. They saw there was a lot of traffic on the old bridge. People of both cities needed another way to cross the Ohio River. The team studied the best way to get the most people and cars across the river.

Engineers used tools to measure the width and depth of the river. They also may have measured how fast the river runs and how high the water rises. After the team measured, it kept good records of its work.

Taking exact measurements is an important part of creating a design. This tool helps the surveyor measure distances and angles.

▶ What problem do you think the surveyor is trying to solve? How might the design process help him?

_____

_____

_____

_____

Planning and Building

The team decided the best solution would be to build another bridge across the Ohio River.

ACTIVE READING As you read these two pages, underline the sentences that describe steps in the design process.

The next step in the design process is to test and improve the prototype. The engineers gather data about important features of the bridge design, such as how stable it is and how much weight it can support. The team may modify minor aspects of the design based on this data.

If the data show that the prototype has significant flaws, the team must start over again. They redesign the bridge by making major changes to their initial plan.

Engineers carefully evaluated and tested the safety of the William H. Natcher Bridge. They made sure that builders followed the plans and used the correct materials.

The last step in the design process is to communicate the solution. Bridge inspectors used their findings, or evidence, to write reports. They used mathematical representations, such as graphs, tables, and drawings, to explain that the bridge was safe to open. Engineers could now use this information to make improvements and build bridges in other places!

The prototype helped builders know how wide, tall, and long to make the bridge.

Communication Is Key!

List three other ways you might communicate the results of a project to others.

_____

_____

How Do Designs Get Better Over Time?

An engineer's work is never done! Every invention can be improved. For example, instead of building a fire in a wood stove or turning on a gas or electric oven, you can use a microwave to cook your food.

Just as with stoves, engineers have come up with newer and better designs for cell phones. Forty years ago, cell phones were bulky and heavy. Today, the smallest cell phone is not much bigger than a watch!

Martin Cooper invented the first cell phone in 1973. It was 13 inches long, weighed about 2 pounds, and allowed only 30 minutes of talk time.

▶ What might happen if cell phones get too small?

_____

_____

_____

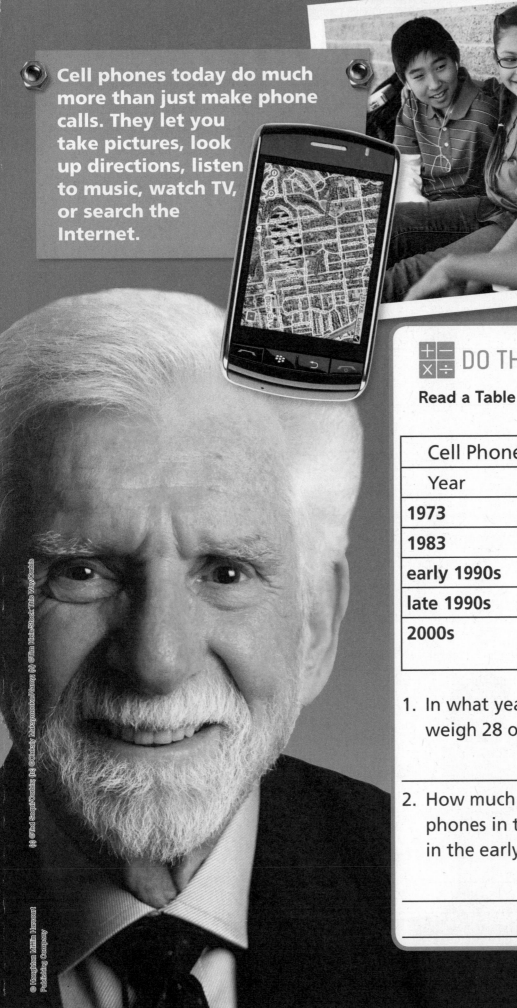

Cell phones today do much more than just make phone calls. They let you take pictures, look up directions, listen to music, watch TV, or search the Internet.

DO THE **MATH**

Read a Table

Cell Phones Over Time	
Year	Weight
1973	about 2 pounds
1983	28 ounces
early 1990s	about 8 ounces
late 1990s	about 4 ounces
2000s	less than 2 ounces

1. In what year did cell phones weigh 28 ounces?

_____

2. How much smaller were phones in the late 1990s than in the early 1990s?

_____

Sum It Up »

Complete the step of the design process in each sentence.

1

1. First, find a _____.

2. Second, _____ and _____ a prototype.

3. Third, _____ and _____ the prototype.

4. Fourth, _____ the prototype as necessary.

5. Fifth, _____ the solution, test data, and your improvements.

Name _____

Vocabulary Review

1 Use the words in the box to complete each sentence.

1. A _____ is a plan for a solution that may use many drawings.

2. When you _____, you let people know about a design.

3. A _____ is something that needs a solution.

4. The steps engineers follow to solve problems is called a _____.

5. To _____ a design means to judge how well it works.

6. The outcome of the design process is a _____.

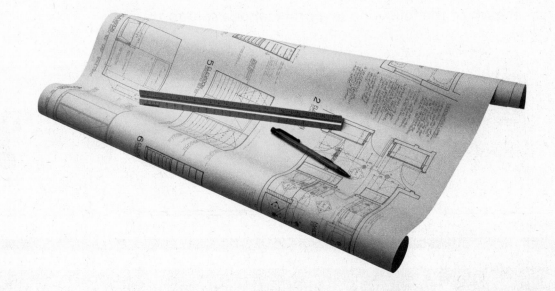

| problem | process | solution | design | evaluate | communicate |

Apply Concepts

2 Kyle's pet hamster is curious! It always finds a way out of its cage. Use the design process to help Kyle solve this problem.

_____

_____

_____

_____

_____

3 Label each of the following as a problem or a solution.

_____   _____   _____   _____

Take It Home! See _ScienceSaurus_® for more information about engineers.

SC.3.N.1.3 Keep records as appropriate, such as pictorial, written, or simple charts and graphs, of investigations conducted. SC.3.N.3.2 Recognize that scientists use models to help understand and explain how things work.

i INQUIRY LESSON 2

Name _____

ESSENTIAL **QUESTION**

How Can You Design a Tree House?

Materials
colored pencils or markers
notebook

EXPLORE

In this activity, you will create a design for a tree house. As part of your planning, you must plan and design a way to move materials. You can follow the steps of the design process to solve these problems.

Before You Begin—Preview the Steps

1. Think about your tree house. One problem is how to move objects from the ground into the tree to build the house.

2. Now come up with a plan and use colored pencils or markers to design, or draw, your tree house. How will you move the materials into the tree?

3. Look carefully at your design. Decide if you need to improve or redesign your plan. Record your final design.

Set a Purpose

What will you do in this activity?

_____

_____

_____

Think About the Procedure

What parts of the design process will you use in this activity?

_____

_____

_____

Why is it important to have a plan before you start building the tree house?

_____

_____

_____

_____

What problems do you identify? How might you solve these problems?

_____

_____

_____

Name _____

Record Your Data

In the space below, draw a prototype for your plan.

Draw Conclusions

Why do you think it is important to build a prototype for your plan before you start building the actual tree house?

_____

_____

_____

Claims • Evidence • Reasoning

1. Suppose you were going to use the design process to build the tree house you've designed. What more would you need to do before you began building? Explain your reasoning.

_____

_____

_____

_____

_____

_____

_____

2. As you look at your prototype and think about it, is there any part you would want to redesign? Give your reasons.

_____

_____

_____

_____

_____

3. What other things would you like to know about how the design process is used to plan projects like your tree house?

_____

_____

_____

_____

SC.3.N.1.4 Recognize the importance of communication among scientists. SC.3.N.1.6 Infer based on observation.

LESSON 3

ESSENTIAL **QUESTION**

How Are Technology and Society Related?

 **Engage Your Brain**

Find the answer to the following question in this lesson and record it here.

Where is the technology in this picture?

_____
_____

_____
_____

ACTIVE **READING**

Lesson Vocabulary

Write the term. As you learn about it, make notes in the Interactive Glossary.

_____

Signal Words: Details

Signal words show connections between ideas. *For example* signals examples of an idea. *Also* signals added facts. Active readers remember what they read because they are alert to signal words that identify examples and facts about a topic.

Technology

What is technology? Look at this train station. Nearly everything you see is an example of technology.

ACTIVE READING As you read these two pages, circle two clue words or phrases that signal a detail such as an example or an added fact.

Technology is anything that people make or do that changes the natural world. Technology meets people's wants or needs. Technology is not just computers and cell phones. Think about the things in a train station. They all have a purpose. The technology in a train station helps people travel easily. Can you imagine how different the world would be without technology?

Suitcase

A suitcase contains a traveler's needs. For example, it can carry clothing, shoes, pajamas, a hairbrush, a toothbrush, and toothpaste. All of these items are examples of technology.

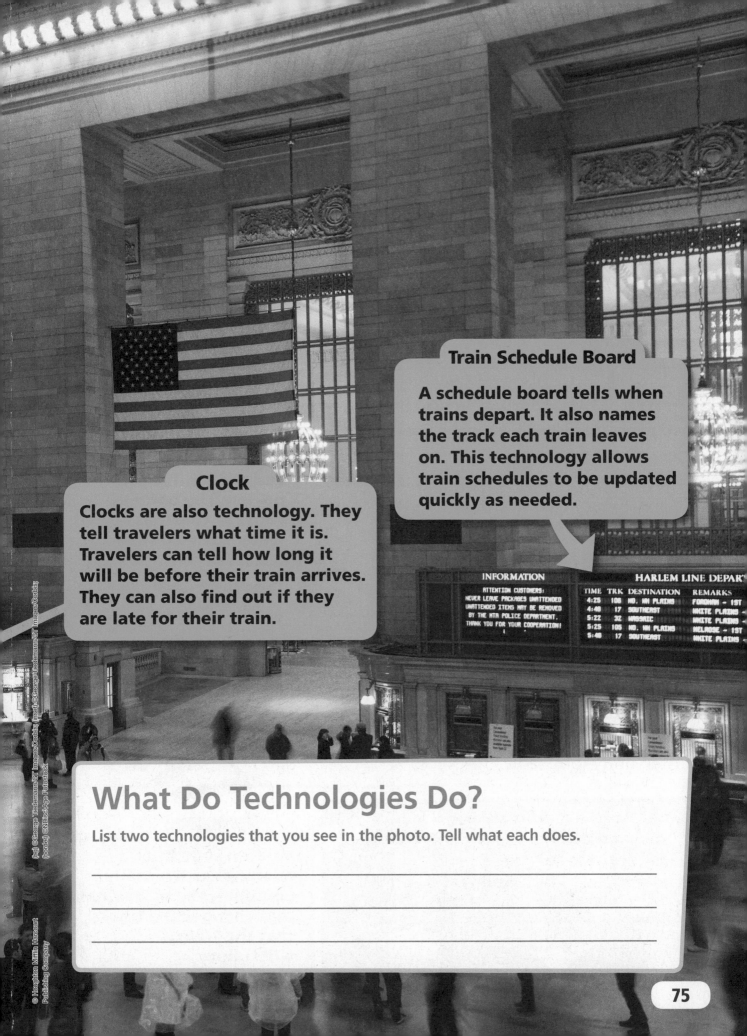

Train Schedule Board

A schedule board tells when trains depart. It also names the track each train leaves on. This technology allows train schedules to be updated quickly as needed.

Clock

Clocks are also technology. They tell travelers what time it is. Travelers can tell how long it will be before their train arrives. They can also find out if they are late for their train.

INFORMATION
ATTENTION CUSTOMERS:
NEVER LEAVE PACKAGES UNATTENDED
UNATTENDED ITEMS MAY BE REMOVED
BY THE MTA POLICE DEPARTMENT.
THANK YOU FOR YOUR COOPERATION!

HARLEM LINE DEPART

TIME	TRK	DESTINATION	REMARKS
4:25	108	NO. WH PLAINS	FORDHAM - 1ST
4:48	17	SOUTHEAST	WHITE PLAINS
5:22	32	HARSAIC	WHITE PLAINS
5:25	105	NO. WH PLAINS	MELROSE - 1ST
5:48	17	SOUTHEAST	WHITE PLAINS

What Do Technologies Do?

List two technologies that you see in the photo. Tell what each does.

_____

_____

_____

Technology Through Time

A train today is different from a train from 100 years ago or even 50 years ago!

Technology is always changing. The earliest trains were dragged along grooves in the ground. Today, superfast trains can travel hundreds of miles an hour. Train tracks have changed over time, too. New technology made tracks of iron. These could carry heavier loads. Trains could be larger and also travel faster. These improvements made trains more useful to people. Improvements in technology make trains work better, faster, and more easily.

Steam locomotive 1800s

Steam locomotives were developed in the early 1800s. They were powered by burning wood or coal that heated water to make steam.

Modern switches operate electronically. Computers send a signal that changes the tracks that the train will follow.

The earliest track switches were moved by hand.

Diesel engine 1900s

By the mid-1900s, the diesel engine had replaced the steam locomotive. Diesel is a type of fuel.

Maglev train 2000s

The fastest trains don't run on tracks anymore. Maglev trains ride on powerful magnets.

DO THE MATH

Interpret a Table

Look at the table. How much faster is the Maglev train than the steam locomotive at maximum speed?

Train Speeds	
Train	Maximum speed (mph)
Steam locomotive	126
Diesel engine	100
Bullet Train	275
Maglev	361

_____

_____

_____

Technology and Society

Technology and society are connected. Technology affects how people live and what they do. People also affect technology by inventing new things.

ACTIVE READING As you read these two pages, put brackets [ ] around the sentence that describes a problem and write *P* next to it. Underline the sentence that describes the solution and write *S* next to it.

Trains are an example of technology's connection to society. Trains carry people and cargo long distances. Resources, such as coal, can be carried long distances in a few days. Before trains, people in California may not have been able to get coal easily. People affect new train technology by finding ways for trains to cross high bridges or to tunnel through mountains. New technology helps trains meet people's needs and wants.

Some cities are far away from where coal is found and steel is produced. Train technology helps resources reach people in faraway cities.

Although trains through the Swiss Alps are safer than trucks on a road, only small trains can pass. The cars, roads, trains, and tracks are all transportation technologies that help people and goods move around the globe.

This new tunnel is beneath the Swiss Alps. The machine behind the workers is a technology that was used to help drill the tunnel. Large trains will be able to use the tunnel. Now people will be able to save more time traveling between cities.

Trains of the Future?

How would you change trains in the future? How would your changes affect society?

_____

_____

_____

_____

_____

Freight trains have refrigerator cars for keeping food fresh. This technology means that food can then be carried safely over long distances.

How Does Technology Affect You?

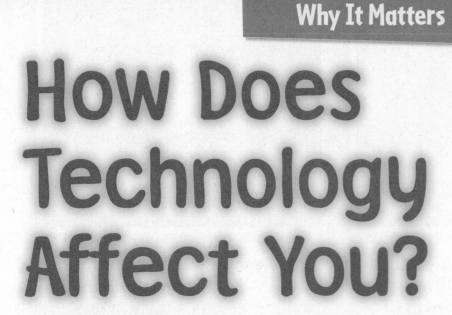

Technologies are always changing. Cars replaced horse-drawn carriages, and maybe someday flying cars will replace the cars we drive today!

ACTIVE READING As you read this page, draw boxes around the names of the things that are being compared.

Think about the technology you use at school and at home. Have you noticed how they have changed? New televisions look different from older ones. Newer computers look much different, too. These newer technologies also do more than their older versions. Technology keeps improving with the goal of making life better.

Cell phone

Do you think when your grandparents were children they had the technology this boy has today?

Technology Changes

This camera uses film, which can store only about 20 images on a roll.

Digital cameras store hundreds of images. Images can be deleted for more space.

Cars in the 1960s used a lot of oil and gas and caused air pollution.

Hybrid cars use both electricity and gas to operate. They cause less air pollution.

Then and Now

Look at the technology below. What can you do with this technology today that people couldn't do 50 years ago?

Earlier telephones had rotary dials and were connected to the wall.

_____

_____

You could not easily edit your work on this typewriter.

_____

_____

Sum It Up »

Complete the summary. Use the information to complete the graphic organizer.

Summarize

Technology is all around you. It can be very simple, like (1) _____.

At a train station, you may see a (2) _____ or a (3) _____.

If you live in a city you may see (4) _____ and (5) _____.

Even in your classroom at school you have a (6) _____, and you may even have a (7) _____.

Main Idea: Technology can be as simple as a fence or as complex as a space station.

(8) Detail: Technology can be complex	(9) Detail: Technology can be simple	Detail: Technology can be simple, like a fence.
_____ _____ _____	_____ _____ _____	

Name _____

Vocabulary Review

1 Write four words from the box that are examples of technology.

fence	giraffe	cell phone	rock
horse	car	leaf	stove

Technology

Apply Concepts

In 2–5, tell which technology you would use and how you would use it.

cell phone

magnifying glass

train

ruler

garden shovel

2 Get the lunch you left at home

_____

_____

_____

3 Visit a friend in another state

_____

_____

4 Plant vegetables in your garden

_____

_____

_____

5 Find out what the fine print on a coupon says

_____

_____

_____

Take It Home!

Share what you have learned about technology with your family. With a family member, make a list of the technology in the kitchen of your home.

SC.3.N.1.3 Keep records as appropriate, such as pictorial, written, or simple charts and graphs, of investigations conducted. SC.3.N.3.2 Recognize that scientists use models to help understand and explain how things work.

INQUIRY LESSON 4

Name _____

ESSENTIAL QUESTION

How Can We Improve a Design?

Materials

- textbooks
- meterstick
- large sheet of construction paper
- toy car
- paper and pencil
- tape and glue
- scissors
- straws
- craft sticks

EXPLORE

Cars travel across bridges every day. What holds them up and makes them strong? How would you design a bridge to support a car?

Before You Begin—Preview the Steps

1. With a partner, set two stacks of books that are both the same height 20 cm apart.

2. Place the construction paper over the gap so that each end of the paper rests on one of the stacks. Push the toy car across the bridge. Observe what happens.

3. Think of a way to improve the design of this bridge. Sketch your ideas with your partner.

4. Build a bridge that matches your design.
   CAUTION: Be careful with scissors!

5. Test your bridge and evaluate your design. Consider ways that you could further improve it.

Set a Purpose

What will you discover in this activity?

_____

_____

_____

Think About the Procedure

How could you and your partner redesign the bridge to make it stronger?

_____

_____

_____

Do you and your partner have different ideas for changing the bridge? Explain.

_____

_____

_____

_____

_____

Name _____

Record Your Data

Sketch your idea for a new bridge design. Make notes about how it differs from the first bridge.

Draw Conclusions

What were the best features of your design? What were the worst features? Explain.

_____

_____

_____

_____

_____

_____

Claims • Evidence • Reasoning

1. Look at the bridges that other students made. What did all the new bridges that worked have in common? Use these observations to write a claim about successful bridges.

_____

_____

_____

2. Cite evidence from the activity that supports your claim and explain why the evidence supports the claim.

_____

_____

_____

_____

_____

_____

3. Why did the first bridge collapse? Explain your reasoning.

_____

_____

_____

4. How could looking at the design of other bridges help you redesign your own bridge?

_____

_____

_____

_____

SC.3.N.1.4 Recognize the importance of communication among scientists.

CAREERS IN SCIENCE

DETOUR

1 Civil engineers plan the structures that are built in cities and towns. Roads and bridges are some of the things they plan.

2 The projects that civil engineers build need to be safe. They must hold up to daily use.

3 Civil engineers improve how we live. They help people get the things they need.

8 Things YOU SHOULD KNOW ABOUT Civil Engineers

4 Civil engineers are important to a growing city or town. They look at the need for new structures.

5 Civil engineers keep cars and trucks moving. They fix roads that are no longer safe.

6 Civil engineers make drawings called construction plans.

7 Civil engineers use tools, such as compasses and rulers. Many engineers use computers.

8 Some civil engineers measure the surface of the land. They use this data to plan buildings.

Engineering Emergency!

Match the problems that can be solved by a civil engineer with its solution in the illustration. Write the number of the problem in the correct triangle on the picture.

1 We have an energy shortage! We can harness the river's energy to generate electricity.

3 The streets are always jammed. We have a transportation crisis!

2 The city is getting crowded! More people are moving here. They need more places to live and work.

4 The nearest bridge is too far away. We need a faster and easier way to get across the river.

Think About It!

If you were a civil engineer, what kind of changes would you make where you live?

_____

_____

Vocabulary Review

Use the terms in the box to complete the sentences.

design process
technology

1. When Ms. Simm's third graders designed a tunnel,

   they followed steps in a _____.

2. A dishwasher is an example of something that makes a family's

   life easier and is a kind of _____.

Science Concepts

Fill in the letter of the choice that best answers the question.

3. The Johnson family decided to purchase a new vehicle. An important feature they searched for was four-wheel drive because four-wheel drive works well in snow. Why is the invention of four-wheel drive a kind of technology?

   Ⓐ It solves the problem of increasing vehicle size.

   Ⓑ It meets the needs of drivers.

   Ⓒ It protects the environment.

   Ⓓ It decreases safety.

4. Stewart will be working with a team to design an improved outdoor light. What should they do before beginning improvements?

   Ⓕ improve their new design

   Ⓖ keep the old design just as it is

   Ⓗ test their new design

   Ⓘ test the old design

5. What is the **main** goal of the design process?

   Ⓐ to find solutions to problems

   Ⓑ to give scientists something to do

   Ⓒ to make charts and graphs

   Ⓓ to write articles for magazines

6. Grace, Miguel, and Amelia are studying how improving technologies can affect the environment. They have to design an invention that affects the environment in a positive way. Which invention do you think they picked?

   Ⓕ a bus that uses more gas than others

   Ⓖ a car tire that cannot be recycled

   Ⓗ an electric train that does not run on fuel

   Ⓘ a new fabric made from rare plants

7. Grocery stores can be very busy places. After people fill up their carts with what they need, they may have to stand in line for a while. The inventor of self-checkout lanes improved technology to help consumers. What new needs could self-checkout lanes cause?

(A) colder freezer and refrigerator sections

(B) automatic-bagging technology

(C) safer pesticide use on produce

(D) improved travel technology

8. Kelsey is researching new computers. She wants to find the computer with the newest technology. Which computer is she most likely to choose?

(F) the biggest computer

(G) the least expensive computer

(H) the oldest computer

(I) the computer with the fastest processing speed

9. What problem did adding air conditioning to cars solve?

(A) Car engines got too hot during the summer.

(B) People got too cold inside cars during the winter

(C) People got too hot inside cars during the summer.

(D) The car radio got too hot during the hot summer days.

10. This is a technology that helped John's grandmother.

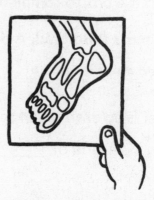

How did this technology most likely help John's grandmother?

(F) It showed his grandmother that she was wearing the wrong size shoe.

(G) It showed his grandmother what type of socks she should wear.

(H) It showed that his grandmother's foot did not have bones.

(I) It showed his grandmother's broken bones.

11. Scientists notice a problem with an engine. It is getting too hot after it runs for a long time. What should the scientists do **next**?

(A) take the engine apart

(B) plan and build a new engine

(C) test and improve the new engine design

(D) communicate results of the new engine design

Name _____

12. An engineer designs a new engine, but one of the parts keeps melting. The engine can get hotter than 240 °C. Look at the table.

Material	Melting Point (°C)
potassium	64
plastic	120
tin	232
aluminum	660

Which material would you suggest the engineer use in the next design?

(F) aluminum

(G) plastic

(H) potassium

(I) tin

13. Suppose you are digging a stone out of the ground with a shovel. You have a problem after you dig all the dirt around the stone. The stone is too heavy to lift. What is your best option in solving this problem?

(A) continue to try lifting it yourself

(B) start over and pick a smaller rock

(C) use a bigger shovel

(D) use a tractor to pull it out of the ground

14. Suppose you are in a tree house you built. You notice that one of the boards is broken and could cause an accident. How could you improve your design?

(F) paint the board with a bright color

(G) replace the board with stronger wood

(H) replace the entire floor

(I) tear down the tree house

15. The chart below shows the number of miles per gallon of gas used by some cars. The cars that use the least gas travel more miles per gallon. How many cars use the least amount of gas?

Gas Mileage Per Gallon of Gasoline

Miles Per Gallon	Tally of Car Models
9–12	I
13–16	III
17–20	HHt
21–25	III
26–30	HHt II
31–34	HHt IIII
35–40	II

Each tally mark represents 1 car model.

(A) 1

(B) 2

(C) 7

(D) 9

Apply Inquiry and Review the Big Idea

Write the answers to these questions.

Use the picture to answer question 16.

16. Write three kinds of technology shown in the scene. Make a claim about how each improves society. Use evidence to support your claim.

_____

_____

_____

17. You move to a new home with a doghouse in the backyard. Your small dog cannot get into the doghouse easily because it is raised up off the ground. What is the problem? What can you do to solve this problem? Explain your reasoning.

_____

_____

_____

The Earth and Stars

FLORIDA **BIG IDEA 5**

Earth in Space and Time

FLORIDA **BIG IDEA 6**

Earth Structures

Stars can be seen in the Florida night sky.

I Wonder Why

From Earth, space looks like this. Astronauts explore this space. Why are astronauts able to travel into space? *Turn the page to find out.*

Here's Why

Astronauts are sent into space in space vehicles. They are still affected by Earth's gravity.

Essential Questions and Florida Benchmarks

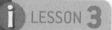

 ## Science Notebook

Before you begin each lesson, write your thoughts about the Essential Question.

SC.3.E.5.1 Explain that stars can be different . . . **SC.3.E.5.2** Identify the Sun as a star that emits energy; some of it in the form of light. **SC.3.E.5.3** Recognize that the Sun appears large and bright because it is the closest star to Earth. **SC.3.E.5.5** Investigate that the number of stars that can be seen through telescopes is dramatically greater . . . **SC.3.E.6.1** Demonstrate that radiant energy from the Sun can heat objects . . .

LESSON **1**

ESSENTIAL **QUESTION**

What Are the Sun and Stars?

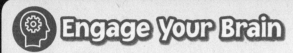

Engage Your Brain

Find the answer to the following question in this lesson and record it here.

How can a star affect Earth?

_____

_____

_____

ACTIVE **READING**

Lesson Vocabulary
List the terms. As you learn about each one, make notes in the Interactive Glossary.

_____

_____

_____

Using Headings
Active readers preview headings and use them to pose questions about the material they will read. Reading to find an answer helps active readers focus on understanding and remembering what they read.

Stars
Up Close!

On a clear night you can see many stars in the sky. By day, you see the sun shining. How are the sun and other stars alike and different?

ACTIVE **READING** As you read these two pages, underline the definition of *sun*.

The Sun

Our **sun** is a medium-size star. The sun appears much larger than other stars. It also appears much brighter. That is because the sun is much closer to Earth than other stars are.

From Earth, our sun looks like a giant ball of light. The sun, like other stars, gives off light and heat.

The way the sun looks close up is very different from the way it looks from Earth.

Stars

A **star** is a ball of hot, glowing gases. From Earth most stars look like small points of light. This is because they are far away. The sun and other stars are both present in the daytime. You cannot see the other stars because the sun makes the sky so bright.

The surface of other stars may look very much like the surface of our sun.

▶ Compare and contrast the sun with one of the stars shown on this page. Tell two ways they are alike and two ways they are different.

Sun	Both Stars	Other Star

Great Balls of Fire

From far away, stars look very similar. Up close, stars have many different characteristics. How are stars alike? How are they different?

ACTIVE **READING** Draw circles around the headings. What are you going to read about stars? Read to see if you were correct.

▶ Use the space below to draw your own star. Describe your star based upon its color, size, and brightness.

(bg) ©NASA, ESA, T. Megeath (University of Toledo) and M. Robberto (STScI)

Stars are born in giant clouds of gas and dust like this one.

Brightness

Brightness tells how much light a star gives off. A very bright star gives off a lot of light. Some stars are much brighter than our sun. Others are dimmer.

Size

Supergiant stars are the largest stars. Hundreds or thousands of our sun could fit inside one supergiant star! The smallest stars are called white dwarfs. Space is filled with many different kinds of beautiful stars!

Color

Stars have different colors. Our sun is a yellow star. Blue, white, and red are other colors of stars. Blue stars are the hottest. Red stars are the coolest.

Full of Energy

Earth would be a cold, dark, and empty planet without the sun. Life could not survive. Read on to find out why.

The Sun Lights Earth

Radiant [RAY•dee•uhnt] energy is energy that can travel through space! Stars give off radiant energy. The sun is our closest star. Some of its radiant energy travels to Earth as light. This light energy helps people and animals see.

Plants use light energy to make their own food. Without light energy from the sun, there could be no plants on Earth. So without the sun, there would be no plants or animals on Earth.

The sun's light makes day brighter than night.

The Sun Heats Earth

Other radiant energy from the sun warms Earth's land, air, and water. During the night, some heat leaves Earth. That is why it is cooler at night than during the day.

You cannot see the sun's energy heating Earth, but you can feel it. When you walk on a beach heated by the sun, the sand feels hot. Without the sun's radiant energy, Earth would be too cold for people to live.

Plants need light to survive.

The sun's energy warms Earth's water.

▶ Draw a picture to show how the sun affects something on Earth.

Stargazing

Away from city lights, you can see thousands of stars in the night sky. You can see many more stars if you use a telescope.

ACTIVE **READING** As you read this page, underline the sentences that tell what a telescope does.

A **telescope** is a tool that makes faraway objects seem larger. It makes faraway objects seem closer, too. With a telescope, you can see many more stars than you can with your eyes. Stars that are bright look even brighter. Stars that are dim look brighter, too.

Even with a telescope, most stars look like points of light in the sky. That's because they are so far away. Only the sun looks different. The sun is much closer to Earth than the other stars. Because the sun is so close to Earth, you should never look directly at it.

A telescope is a long tube with lenses at both ends. The lenses make objects appear larger and closer.

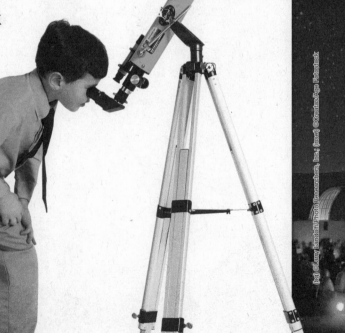

With a telescope, stars look brighter and clearer.

You can see many stars with just your eyes.

 DO THE MATH

Solve a Word Problem

Max looks at a part of the sky through a hollow tube. He counts 8 stars. Then he looks at the sky with a telescope. He sees 5 times as many stars. How many stars does Max see now?

_____

Sum It Up »

Read the summary statements below. Each one is incorrect.
Change the circled part of the summary to make it correct.

1 The sun is a star that gives off light and (electric energy.)
_____

2 Stars look like (flashes) of light in the night sky.
_____

3 You can see (fewer) stars with a telescope than with just your eyes.
_____

4 The sun is a ball of hot, glowing (clouds.)
_____

5 Stars are grouped by their color, brightness, and (shape.)
_____

Name _____

Vocabulary Review

1 Use the clues to unscramble the words in the boxes.

| rats | _____ | A ball of hot, glowing gases |

| gtilh | _____ | The kind of energy from the sun that helps people |

| pelsectoe | _____ | An instrument that makes stars look brighter and closer |

| usn | _____ | The star that is closest to Earth |

| trindaa | _____ | The kind of energy that can move through space |

| oolrc | _____ | A feature of stars in addition to brightness and size |

Apply Concepts

2 Draw stars you might see with your eyes. Then draw stars you might see with a telescope.

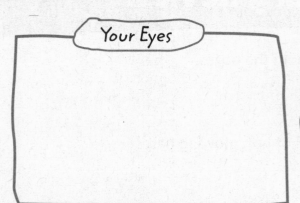

Your Eyes   A Telescope

3 Think about the characteristics of stars. Draw one. Describe its color, size, and brightness.

_____

_____

4 The sun shines on the town in the picture. Tell some of the ways that the sun affects this town.

_____

_____

_____

_____

Take It Home!

See *ScienceSaurus*® for more information about the solar system.

SC.3.E.5.1 Explain that stars can be different . . . SC.3.E.5.5 Investigate that the number of stars that can be seen through telescopes is dramatically greater than those seen by the unaided eye. SC.3.N.3.2 Recognize the scientists use model . . . SC.3.N.3.3 Recognize that all models are approximations of natural phenomena.

i INQUIRY
LESSON **2**

Name _____

ESSENTIAL **QUESTION**

How Many Stars Do You See?

Materials

box with pinholes on one side

small lamp without a shade

hand lens

EXPLORE

Let's go stargazing! In this activity, you and your classmates will model the night sky. You will count and describe the "stars" you see.

Before You Begin—Preview the Steps

1 Watch as your teacher places the box over the lamp. Turn off the lights in your classroom. Move far away from the box.

2 Observe the points of light. Count and record how many you see.

3 Move closer to the box. Observe the points of light again. Count and record how many you see.

4 Move closer to the box. Use a hand lens to observe the box. Record your observations.

Set a Purpose

What do you think you will learn from observing the box with pinholes?

_____

_____

_____

_____

Think About the Procedure

Why do you think you are observing the points of light from different distances?

_____

_____

_____

_____

Name _____

Record Your Data

In the space below, make a data table to record what you observe.
Compare your data with data collected by your classmates.

Draw Conclusions

How were the points of light you observed different from far away, from close up, and through the hand lens?

_____

_____

_____

_____

Claims • Evidence • Reasoning

1. Think about your observations. Write a claim about what you would see if you moved even closer to the box.

   _____

   _____

   _____

2. Cite evidence from the activity that supports your claim and explain why the evidence supports the claim.

   _____

   _____

   _____

   _____

   _____

3. In the box below, draw what a point of light looked like from a distance. Then draw what it looked like when it was closer.

4. For what tool is the hand lens a model? How is the model like that tool?

   _____

   _____

   _____

   _____

SC.3.E.6.1 Demonstrate that radiant energy from the Sun can heat objects and when the Sun is not present, heat may be lost. **SC.3.N.1.5** Recognize that scientists question, discuss, and check each other's evidence and explanations.

ⓘ **INQUIRY LESSON 3**

Name _____

ESSENTIAL QUESTION

How Does the Sun Heat Earth?

Materials
- 1 thermometer per group
- 1 cup per group
- soil

EXPLORE

It's a bright and sunny day outside. The air feels hot. Some days are hotter than others. The sun's energy affects Earth in different ways. In this activity, you will explore one way that radiant energy from the sun affects Earth.

Before You Begin—Preview the Steps

① Use one cup and one thermometer for your group. Fill your cup with soil. Place the thermometer in the cup. Record the temperature.

② Place your group's cup either in the sun or in the shade, as instructed by your teacher.

③ Check your group's thermometer every hour for 2 hours. Observe and record each temperature.

④ Some groups will move their cups from the sunshine to the shade. Keep recording the temperature of your group's cup every hour for 3 more hours.

113

Set a Purpose
What will you learn from this activity?

_____

_____

_____

Think About the Procedure
Why do you think some students move their cup from the sunny spot into the shade?

_____

_____

_____

_____

Name _____

Record Your Data

Use your Science Notebook. Record the temperatures in a data table. Use it to make a bar graph here.

Draw Conclusions

How did the bar graph help you communicate your data?

_____

_____

_____

Claims • Evidence • Reasoning

1. Interpret your data. Write a claim about how the heat from the sun affected the soil in the cups.

_____

_____

Claims • Evidence • Reasoning (continued)

2. Cite evidence from the activity that supports your claim and explain why the evidence supports the claim.

_____

_____

_____

_____

3. Share the data in your bar graphs. Write a claim about which thermometer showed the greatest increase in temperature.

_____

4. What happened to the thermometer that was moved into the shade? Why do you think this happened? Explain your reasoning.

_____

_____

_____

5. Draw a way that radiant energy from the sun affects organisms on Earth.

SC.3.E.5.1 Explain that stars can be different; some are smaller, some are larger, and some appear brighter than others; all except the Sun are so far away that they look like points of light. **SC.3.N.1.5** Recognize that scientists question, discuss, and check each others' evidence and explanations.

 PEOPLE **IN SCIENCE**

Meet the Stargazers

Ellen Ochoa

In school, Ellen Ochoa loved math and science. Ochoa worked hard in school and became a scientist. She invented optical equipment that can help explore objects in space. She used a robotic arm to work with machines in space. In 1991, Ochoa was the first Hispanic woman to become an astronaut.

On a space flight, Ochoa used a robotic arm to capture an orbiting telescope.

Subrahmanyan Chandrasekhar

Subrahmanyan Chandrasekhar studied how stars change. He discovered that stars can be many different sizes. Some stars slowly become cool. Others collapse into a black hole. Scientists questioned his discovery, but years later accepted it. In 1983, Chandrasekhar won the Nobel Prize for his work with stars.

The collapse of a star can form a black hole. In a black hole, light cannot es-

Crossword Puzzle

astronaut	optical	black hole	size	Ochoa	Prize

Read each clue and write the answer in the correct squares.

Across

1. where light cannot escape
3. Chandrasekhar was awarded the Nobel _____.
4. a person trained to work in space

Down

2. Ochoa invented _____ equipment.
5. Stars can be different in _____.
6. first Hispanic woman astronaut

SC.3.E.5.4 Explore the Law of Gravity by demonstrating that gravity is a force that can be overcome.

LESSON **4**

ESSENTIAL **QUESTION**

What Is Gravity?

 Engage Your Brain

Find the answer to the following question in this lesson and record it here.

Why are these skydivers falling toward Earth?

_____

_____

_____

📖 ACTIVE **READING**

Lesson Vocabulary

List the terms. As you learn about each one, make notes in the Interactive Glossary.

_____

_____

Cause and Effect

Some ideas in this lesson are connected by a cause-and-effect relationship. What makes something happen is a cause. What happens because of something else is an effect. Active readers look for effects by asking themselves, What happened? They look for causes by asking, Why did it happen?

Gravity!

If you let go of a basketball, it will not stay in the air. It falls to the ground. What makes it fall?

ACTIVE **READING** As you read this page, draw one line under a cause. Draw two lines under an effect.

Objects fall because a force pulls them to the ground. A **force** is a push or a pull. The force that causes objects to fall is called gravity. **Gravity** is a force that pulls objects toward one another. It pulls objects toward Earth. If you jump into the air, gravity will pull you back to Earth. Because of gravity's pull, the planets travel in paths around the sun.

What goes up, must come down. That's because of gravity!

▶ Draw some examples of gravity at work that you have seen today.

You may not think about it, but you see how gravity works every day. These photos show gravity at work.

The penguin in the top photo is diving off a cliff. It doesn't hang in the air, and it doesn't float up! Gravity pulls the penguin down toward Earth and into the water.

In the bottom photo, kids are going down a slide. Gravity pulls them toward Earth. The slide keeps them from falling straight down.

Gravity helps this penguin quickly get into the water.

These kids are using gravity to have some fun!

Stop it!

The kids on the previous page do not fall straight down. Instead, they slide safely to the ground. The slide changes the effect of gravity on their motion.

ACTIVE **READING** read these two pages, circle examples of objects that can overcome gravity.

You know that gravity is a force. Other forces can *oppose*, or act against, gravity. Picture a baseball player catching a fly ball in his mitt. The mitt stops the ball from falling to the ground. Gravity has been opposed.

When you catch a falling ball, you balance gravity's pull.

The force of this rocket opposes gravity. The force is strong enough for the rocket to leave the ground.

This skywalk hangs over the Grand Canyon. It pushes up on people's feet. The force is strong enough to keep people from falling into the canyon below.

The air pushes up on this hang glider. The push of the air opposes the pull of gravity.

The pictures on these pages show more ways that gravity can be opposed. Look at the hang glider. Air pushes up on the glider. Because this upward force opposes gravity, the hang glider does not fall to Earth. The rocket in the picture on the previous page works against Earth's gravity. The rocket goes up into the sky. It takes a force greater than the force of Earth's gravity to launch the rocket.

Keep It Up!

What are some ways you can overcome gravity? Make a list.

_____

_____

_____

_____

Sum It Up »

Complete the summary. Use the information to complete the graphic organizer.

A push or pull is a **(1)** _____. Gravity is a kind of force. It pulls objects toward each other. Gravity is what holds objects on **(2)** _____. Sometimes people can overcome **(3)** _____. For example, a person can catch a ball in the air. A rocket can be launched. A person can soar in a hang glider.

Summarize

Main Idea: Gravity is a force that pulls objects toward Earth, but other forces can oppose gravity.

Detail: (4)	Detail: (5)	Detail: Gravity enables a bird to dive.
_____	_____	
_____	_____	
_____	_____	
_____	_____	
_____	_____	

Name _____

Vocabulary Review

**Look at the picture clues. Fill in the correct term.
Circle the letters with numbers underneath them.**

1

The ball is pulled by

__ __ __ __ __ __ __
    8   6

2

A push or a pull

__ __ __ __ __
  5   1

3

A kind of force

__ __ __ __ __
 3 2

4

Gravity is

__ __ __ __ __ __ __
           4   7

5 Look at the letters in circles. Match the letter with
the number below each space. Then solve the riddle.

What is an astronaut's favorite drink?

A __ __ __ __ __   G R A V I-__ __ __
   1 2 3 4 5   6 7 8

Apply Concepts

Is gravity being opposed? Write *yes* or *no*.

 6    **7**    **8**

_____   _____   _____

9 Look at the picture below. Describe how the rocket opposes the force of gravity.

_____

_____

_____

_____

_____

_____

_____

SC.3.N.1.7 Explain that empirical evidence is information, such as observations or measurements, that is used to help validate explanations of natural phenomena.

S.T.E.M.
ENGINEERING & TECHNOLOGY

How It Works:

Keck Observatory

An observatory is a kind of system. It has many parts that work together. Scientists use observatories to study space. Read about the parts of the Keck Observatory in Hawaii.

The Keck Observatory has two telescopes. Both are as tall as eight-story buildings!

The dome protects the telescope's mirrors from rain and sunlight.

An opening in the dome turns to show different areas of the sky.

The 10-meter main mirror is a powerful magnifier. It is made up of smaller mirrors.

Can You Fix It?

Each part of a system plays a role. If one part breaks, the system may not work. The picture below shows the telescope's main mirror.

Trace the path of the light through the telescope by following the red arrows in the image below.

This planet was photographed by the Keck Observatory.

What would happen if one part of the mirror broke? How could you fix the telescope if this happened?

_____

_____

_____

_____

_____

Owner's Manual:
Using a Telescope

Have you ever looked through a telescope? If so, you know that a telescope makes distant objects appear closer.

Suppose someone had never used a telescope before. Could you explain how to observe the moon using this tool?

DESIGN PROCESS STEPS

1 Find a Problem
2 Plan & Build
3 Test & Improve
4 Redesign
5 Communicate

What to Do:

1 Learn how telescopes help us observe distant objects.

2 Make a drawing of a telescope.

3 Label the telescope parts.

4 Plan the owner's manual. What main sections will you include?

5 Write a two-page, step-by-step owner's manual that explains how to use this tool to observe the moon in your Science Notebook.

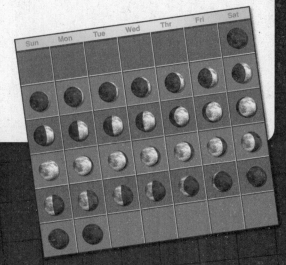

Name _____

Vocabulary Review

Use the terms in the box to complete the sentences.

force
gravity
star

1. A(n) _____ is a ball of hot, glowing gases that makes its own light.

2. A(n) _____ is a push or a pull.

3. A force that pulls objects toward one another and pulls objects toward Earth is _____.

Science Concepts

Fill in the letter of the choice that best answers the question.

4. Marta had a picnic. She placed one bag of ice on a table in the shade and another bag in the sun. Both bags were the same size and shape. The ice placed in the sun melted more quickly. Why?

Ⓐ The bags of ice were different types.

Ⓑ A summer day is usually warmer than a winter day.

Ⓒ One table was larger than the other.

Ⓓ Things heat up more quickly in the sun than in the shade.

5. Two students want to sit outside in a place that is the coolest from 11:00 a.m. to 1:00 p.m. One thinks a shady spot will be cooler, but the other thinks a sunny spot would be just as cool. How could they use two thermometers to find out?

Ⓕ Compare the temperatures of the shady spot and a classroom from 11:00 a.m. to 1:00 p.m.

Ⓖ Compare the temperatures of the sunny spot and a classroom from 11:00 a.m. to 1:00 p.m.

Ⓗ Compare the temperatures of the shady spot and the sunny spot from 11:00 a.m. to 1:00 p.m.

Ⓘ Compare the temperature of the shady spot from 11:00 a.m. to 1:00 p.m. with its temperature from 9:00 a.m. to 11:00 a.m.

6. Tommy and Maura record how many hours of sunlight they received on the first day of summer. Tommy lives in Alaska. Maura lives in Florida. How could they double-check their own data?

Ⓐ Record the hours again on the first day of winter.

Ⓑ Record the hours again from their own homes.

Ⓒ Go to each other's house and record the hours again.

Ⓓ Go to Texas and record the hours of sunlight together.

7. Joel knows the sun's radiant energy travels through space to Earth. Which is **not** an effect of radiant energy on Earth?

Ⓕ It causes Earth's land to heat up.

Ⓖ It causes Earth's oceans to heat up.

Ⓗ It causes objects to fall to Earth.

Ⓘ It lights up the daytime sky.

8. Liam wants to observe stars in the night sky. Which tool would be **most** helpful?

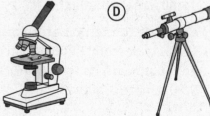
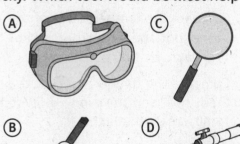

Ⓐ   Ⓒ

Ⓑ   Ⓓ

9. One way scientists classify stars is by color. Blue stars are the hottest. Red stars are the coolest. The sun is a yellow star. Which statement is true?

Ⓕ The sun is cooler than a red star.

Ⓖ The sun is hotter than a blue star.

Ⓗ The sun is hotter than a red star.

Ⓘ All stars have the same temperature.

10. Keisha wants to model how a telescope works. Which could she use as a model?

Ⓐ microscope   Ⓒ hand lens

Ⓑ telescope   Ⓓ goggles

11. A class uses a black box with pinholes and a lamp to model a night sky. They will count the stars from two distances. Which observation gives the **most** details about the stars?

Ⓕ I saw the same number of stars both times I looked.

Ⓖ I counted 6 large, 11 medium, and 7 small stars on the box.

Ⓗ I saw stars in patterns of circles, squares, and rectangles.

Ⓘ I counted by making marks on a separate piece of paper for each star.

12. Hannah notices that the stars and the sun appear very different. Which statement **best** tells why other stars appear different from the sun?

Ⓐ The stars are not as hot as the sun.

Ⓑ The stars are smaller than the sun.

Ⓒ The stars are closer to Earth.

Ⓓ The stars are farther from Earth.

Name _____

13. Which is an example of overcoming gravity?

(F) falling into a pool

(G) dropping a ball

(H) skiing down a hill

(I) catching a baseball

14. Grant jumps into the air. Why does he come back down?

(A) He did not jump on a trampoline.

(B) He did not jump with tennis shoes on.

(C) There is not enough air between his feet and the ground.

(D) There is no force that overcomes gravity's force on him.

15. This picture shows stars in a night sky.

What information can you discover by looking at the picture?

(F) Brighter stars are closest to Earth.

(G) The smallest stars are the brightest.

(H) The largest stars are part of the sun.

(I) Stars look different from one another.

16. The dotted line in the figure shows the path of a thrown stick.

Why does the path curve?

(A) Gravity is pulling the stick down.

(B) The dog is pulling the stick down.

(C) The person used a curve-ball throw.

(D) The air pushes down on the stick.

17. Ally wants to use a model to show her class that the sun appears larger than other stars because it is closer to Earth. What could she use as her model?

(F) a drawing of a large star and the sun

(G) two foam balls of the same size

(H) a picture of the sun next to a picture of a star

(I) a model of the sun, Earth, and other planets

Apply Inquiry and Review the Big Idea

Write the answers to these questions.

18. Marisa uses a black box with pinholes of different sizes to model the night sky. Make a claim about why the box is not a good model for the night sky. Support your claim with evidence and explain how the evidence supports the claim.

_____

_____

_____

19. Imagine that there was suddenly no gravity on Earth. Make a claim about what would most likely happen to a picture hanging on a nail. Explain your reasoning.

_____

_____

20. A weather forecaster measures the air temperature in Tampa. The graph shows her data from 9:00 p.m. to 5:00 a.m.

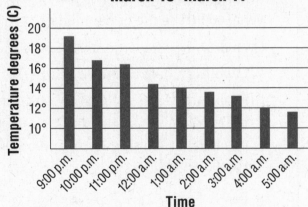

Tampa, FL Overnight Temperatures March 10–March 11

What is a claim you can make based on evidence in the graph? Explain how the evidence supports the claim.

_____

_____

Properties of Matter

A variety of plants live in Florida swamps.

FLORIDA **BIG IDEA** 8

Properties of Matter

FLORIDA **BIG IDEA** 9

Changes in Matter

I Wonder Why

The colors of swamp plants can help us learn how to use properties of matter. Why is this so? *Turn the page to find out.*

Here's Why

Color is a physical property of matter. You can use color to sort plants into groups.

Essential Questions and Florida Benchmarks

 Science Notebook

Before you begin each lesson, write your thoughts about the Essential Question.

SC.3.P.8.1 Measure and compare temperatures of various samples of solids and liquids. SC.3.P.8.2 Measure and compare the mass and volume of solids and liquids. SC.3.P.8.3 Compare materials and objects according to properties such as size, shape, color, texture, and hardness.

LESSON 1

ESSENTIAL QUESTION

What Are Some Physical Properties?

Engage Your Brain

Find the answer to the question in this lesson and record it here.

How can you compare these beach umbrellas?

_____

_____

_____

📖 ACTIVE READING

Lesson Vocabulary

List the terms, and make notes in the Interactive Glossary as you learn more.

_____

_____

_____

_____

_____

Compare and Contrast

Many ideas in this lesson are connected because they explain comparisons and contrasts—how things are alike and different. Active readers stay focused on comparisons and contrasts when they ask themselves, How are things alike? How are they different?

It's Everything!

What is matter? Everything you see on this page is matter. All the "stuff" around you is matter.

ACTIVE **READING** As you read the next page, draw a line under each main idea.

Texture is the way something feels. Objects can be smooth or rough. What is the texture of sand?

_____

_____

Matter can be different colors. Write a sentence that describes the color of the beach ball.

_____

_____

(bkgd) ©ThinkStock/Age Fotostock; (cl) ©Alamy Images Royalty-Free

Matter is anything that takes up space. Your science book takes up more space than your pencil does. Did you know that no two things can take up the same space?

You describe matter by naming its physical properties. A **physical property** is a characteristic of matter that you can observe or measure directly. Look in the boxes to learn about some properties of matter.

Even we are made of matter!

Hardness describes how easily an object's shape can be changed. Name a hard object you see.

_____

_____

_____

_____

Size is how big something is. Which object is the biggest? Which one takes up the most space?

_____

_____

Shape is the form an object has. What words can you use to describe the two smallest shells?

_____

_____

_____

How Much Mass?

Why is it so difficult to lift a bucket full of water? Would it be easier to carry the water in smaller containers instead?

ACTIVE **READING** As you read these two pages, find and underline the definition of mass. Then circle the name of the tool we use to measure mass.

Mass is the amount of matter an object has. Mass is also a measure of how hard it is to move an object. The more mass an object has, the harder it is to move the object.

How can you measure the mass of sand, water, or other materials in a bucket? Check out the next page.

Measure It!

We use a pan balance to measure mass. The pan balance measures mass in grams (g). How can you measure the mass of the contents of a bucket? To find the mass, you have to use math.

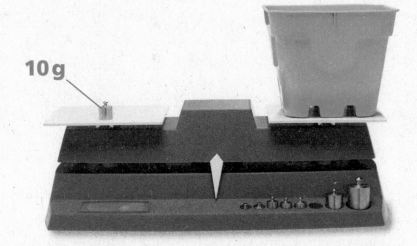

Find the mass of the container alone. _____

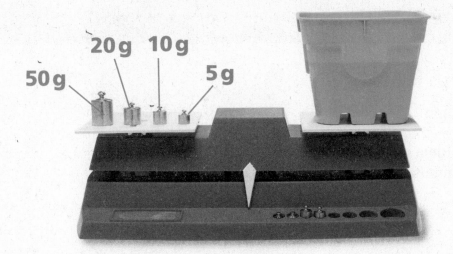

Find the mass of the container + contents. _____

Now you subtract to find the mass of the contents.

Mass of the container + contents	**−**	Mass of the container	**=**	Mass of the contents
_____		_____		_____

What's the Volume?

Matter takes up space. How can you measure the amount of space an object takes up?

ACTIVE READING As you read the next page, circle the name of a tool you can use to measure volume. Underline the units it uses.

An object's **volume** is the amount of space it takes up. To find the volume of a cube or a rectangular [rek•TAN•gyuh•luhr]solid, multiply its length by its width and its height. The length, width, and height of the small cube below are one centimeter.

⊞ DO THE MATH

Find the Volume

This cube's volume is one cubic centimeter.

1 cm

1 cm   1 cm

Find the volume of this cube.

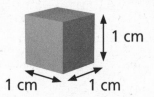

2 cm

2 cm   2 cm

_____ x _____ x _____ = _____ cubic centimeters
  L   W   H

Use a graduated cylinder to measure the volume of a liquid. The units are in milliliters (mL). You can also use it to find the volume of a solid.

Measure It!

Read the level of the water in the graduated cylinder. This is the volume of the water.

_____

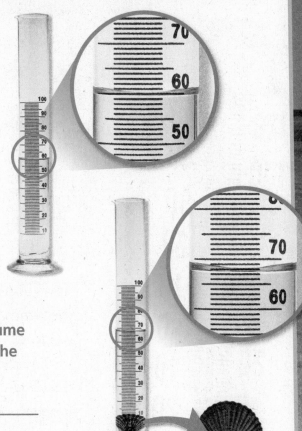

Add a shell and read the volume again. This is the volume of the water + the shell.

_____

Now subtract to find the volume of the shell. The volume of a solid is measured in cubic centimeters. 1 milliliter equals 1 cubic centimeter, so just change *milliliters* to *cubic centimeters.*

volume of water + shell   volume of water   volume of shell

_____ - _____ = _____

Hot and Cold

At the beach, you can feel the difference between hot sand and cold water. How do you measure how warm something is?

Temperature is a measure of how warm something is. You use a thermometer to measure temperature.

Thermometers use a scale of numbers to show temperature. There are two scales that are frequently used.

Most weather reports use the Fahrenheit [FAIR•uhn•hyt] scale. On this scale, water becomes ice at 32 degrees. Water boils at 212 degrees.

The other scale is the Celsius [SEL•see•uhs] scale. On this scale, water becomes ice at 0 degrees. Water boils at 100 degrees.

What temperature does the thermometer show?

_____

_____

Measure It!

Write the air temperature and water temperature on the lines. Then color the thermometer to show the temperature of the sand.

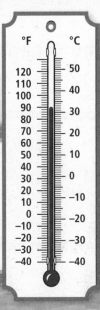

Air Temperature

_____ degrees Celsius

_____ degrees Fahrenheit

You can feel the sand's higher temperature and the water's lower temperature.

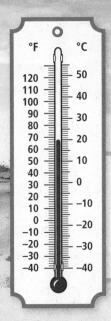

Water Temperature

_____ degrees Celsius

_____ degrees Fahrenheit

Sand Temperature

The sand's temperature is 37 degrees Celsius. Show that temperature on the thermometer.

Sum It Up »

Write the vocabulary term that matches the picture and caption.

1
This crab takes up space and has mass.

_____

2
The blue color is a characteristic of the kite.

_____

3
This manatee has a large amount of matter.

_____

4
This umbrella takes up a lot of space.

_____

5
This thermometer tells how hot it is today.

_____

Name _____

Vocabulary Review

1 Write four words from the box to complete this word web about the physical properties of matter.

| mass | volume | thermometer | color | milliliters | temperature |

_____

_____

Physical Properties

_____

_____

Apply Concepts

In questions 2–4, write the name of the measurement tool you would use.

 2 Degrees Celsius

 3 Milliliters

 4 Grams

Is one drink colder than the other?

_____

Which cup holds the most liquid?

_____

Does a glass of milk have more matter than a glass of punch?

_____

5 Choose an object in your classroom. Write as many physical properties as you can to describe it.

_____

_____

 Take It Home! See *ScienceSaurus*® for more information about physical properties.

Ask a Metallurgist

gold bars

aluminum foil

Now It's Your Turn!

▶ What properties make steel a good material to use for building bridges?

_____

_____

_____

Q. What is a metallurgist?

A. A metallurgist is a scientist who works with metals. Iron, aluminum, gold, and copper are just some of these metals. They also combine different metals to make a new metal.

Q. Why do they combine different metals?

A. Metals may have different weights, strengths, and hardnesses. They combine metals to change their properties. The new metal may be stronger, harder, or a different color.

Q. How do they use the properties of metals in their work?

A. They look at the properties of metals and how metals can be used. Iron is strong. Mixed with other materials it becomes steel. Steel is a hard and strong metal. Copper can conduct electricity. It's a good metal to use for electrical wires.

copper pennies

This Leads to That

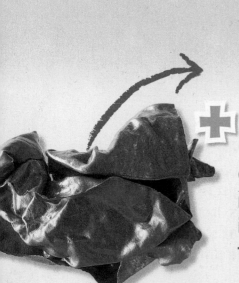

Copper is a soft, red metal. It can be shaped into things and over time turns green.

Tin is a silvery–white metal. It's both flexible and brittle.

Bronze is made by mixing tin and copper. The gold metal is hard and strong. Over time bronze turns green.

Compare the properties of copper and bronze. Then complete the table.

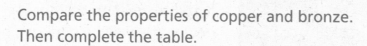

Properties of copper	Properties of both	Properties of bronze

Bronze is shaped to make sculptures and bells.

SC.3.P.8.2 Measure and compare the mass and volume of solids and liquids. **SC.3.N.1.3** Keep records as appropriate, such as pictorial, written, or simple charts and graphs, of investigations conducted.

INQUIRY LESSON 2

Name _____

ESSENTIAL QUESTION

How Are Mass and Volume Measured?

Materials

pan balance
metric ruler
graduated cylinder
measuring cup
water
various solid objects

EXPLORE

Time to measure! In this activity, you and your classmates will measure mass and volume.

Before You Begin—Preview the Steps

1. Gather your materials.

2. Make a table to record your data. You will find the mass and volume of solid objects and a given amount of water.

3. Use a pan balance to find the mass of each. Record your measurements.

4. Find the volume of each. Record your measurements.

Set a Purpose

What skills will you learn?

_____

_____

_____

Think About the Procedure

How can you find the volume of a small object?

_____

_____

_____

_____

_____

When finding the mass of water in a graduated cylinder, why must you first find the mass of the empty graduated cylinder?

_____

_____

_____

_____

Name _____

Record Your Data

Measure the volume and mass of the water and objects.
Make a table to record your results.

Draw Conclusions

When you used water to find the volume of one or more of the objects, how did the volumes of the objects and the water compare?

_____

_____

_____

Claims • Evidence • Reasoning

1. Interpret your data. Write a claim about how the masses of the objects compared. Cite evidence that supports your claim and explain why the evidence supports the claim.

_____

_____

2. Interpret your data. Write a claim about how the volumes of the objects compared. Cite evidence that supports your claim and explain why the evidence supports the claim.

_____

_____

_____

3. Two cubes are made of the same material, but one has a greater volume. Does the larger cube have more mass? Explain your reasoning.

_____

_____

_____

4. A friend collects rocks that fit in the same-sized space in a tray. Could these rocks each have a different volume? Explain your reasoning.

_____

_____

_____

5. Did all the groups in your class have the same results? How can you explain any differences?

_____

_____

_____

SC.3.P.8.1 Measure and compare temperatures of various samples of solids and liquids.
SC.3.N.1.3 Keep records as appropriate, such as pictorial, written, or simple charts and graphs, of investigations conducted. SC.3.N.1.6 Infer based on observation.

 INQUIRY LESSON 3

Name _____

ESSENTIAL QUESTION

How Is Temperature Measured?

Materials

- thermometer
- cup of rice
- cup of sand
- cup of ice
- cup of warm water (Water #1)
- cup of cold water (Water #2)

EXPLORE

You have seen that we use thermometers to measure temperature. You can measure temperature in degrees Fahrenheit or degrees Celsius. Be sure to look at your thermometer to see which one you will use.

Before You Begin—Preview the Steps

1. Make a data table that lists what is in each cup. Leave room to write the temperature of each.

2. Find the temperature of the contents of the first cup. Record a temperature in both the degrees Fahrenheit and the degrees Celsius columns of your table.

3. Do the same for each cup.

Set a Purpose

What skills will you learn from this investigation?

_____

_____

_____

Think About the Procedure

How can you find the temperature of a solid?

_____

_____

Name _____

Record Your Data

Make a table to record your temperature readings.

Draw Conclusions

Use your temperature measurements to list the substances in order from coolest to warmest.

_____

_____

_____

Claims • Evidence • Reasoning

1. Write a claim about the relationship between an object's temperature and whether it feels cool or warm. Cite evidence from your observations and explain how it supports your claim.

_____

_____

_____

_____

2. How did the temperatures you measured compare with the temperatures measured by others? Explain any differences.

_____

_____

_____

3. Why do you think cooks use thermometers in the kitchen? Explain your reasoning.

_____

_____

_____

_____

4. How could you find out if the air temperature given in your local weather report is correct?

_____

_____

5. Think of other questions you would like to ask about measuring temperature.

_____

_____

SC.3.P.9.1 Describe the changes water undergoes when it changes state through heating and cooling by using familiar scientific terms such as melting, freezing, boiling, evaporation, and condensation.

LESSON 4

ESSENTIAL QUESTION
What Are the States of Matter?

🧠 Engage Your Brain

Find the answer to the following question in this lesson and record it here.

How does heating this frozen treat affect it?

_____

_____

📖 ACTIVE READING

Lesson Vocabulary
List the terms, and make notes in the Interactive Glossary as you learn more.

_____

_____

_____

_____

_____

Signal words show connections between ideas. Words signaling a cause include *because* and *if*. Words signaling an effect include *so* and *thus*. Active readers remember what they read because they are alert to signal words that identify causes and effects.

What's the State?

What a party! You can eat a piece of solid cake, drink a cold liquid, or play with a gas-filled balloon.

ACTIVE READING As you read these two pages, draw circles around the names of the three states of matter that are being compared.

There are three common states of matter. They are solid, liquid, and gas. Water can be found in all three states.

A **solid** is matter that takes up a definite amount of space. A solid also has a definite shape. Your science book is a solid. Ice is also a solid.

A **liquid** is matter that also takes up a definite amount of space, but it does not have a definite shape. Liquids take the shape of their containers. Drinking water is a liquid.

A **gas** is matter that does not take up a definite amount of space and does not have a definite shape. The air around you is a gas.

curtains _____

ribbon _____

ice cubes _____

orange drink _____

▶ Identify the solids, liquids, and gases in the picture by writing *S*, *L*, or *G* in each box.

air in balloon _____

bubbles _____

plastic _____

Cool! It's Freezing!

Water freezes at 0 °C.

When matter cools, it loses energy.
How does cooling affect water?

ACTIVE READING As you read these two pages, draw circles around the clue words that signal a cause-and-effect relationship.

All the pictures show water at a temperature lower than 0 degrees Celsius (0 °C) or 32 degrees Fahrenheit (32 °F). How do we know this? If liquid water cools to that temperature, it freezes. Below that temperature, water exists as a solid—ice. Freezing is the change of state from a liquid to a solid.

How would this igloo be different if its temperature was 10 °C?

_____

_____

How can you tell that the temperature of the snow is below 0 °C?

_____

_____

Hail is water that falls to Earth as small balls of ice.

This snowball holds together because the water in it is frozen into a solid.

This girl can skate on ice because ice is a solid.

 DO THE **MATH**

Solve a Story Problem

The temperature of a puddle of water is 10 °C. The water cools by two degrees every hour. In how many hours will the puddle of water begin to freeze? Explain how you got your answer.

_____

_____

_____

_____

Just Add Heat!

When matter is heated, it gains energy.
How can heating affect water?

ACTIVE **READING** As you read the next page, draw one
line under a cause. Draw two lines under the effect.

Water is a liquid between
the temperatures of 0 °C
and 100 °C.

If the sun heats this ice
sculpture enough, it will
begin to melt.

What happens to an ice cube after you take it
from the freezer? As it warms, it begins to melt.
Melting is the change of state from a solid to a
liquid. Ice melts at the same temperature that liquid
water freezes—0 °C (32 °F). Melting is the opposite
of freezing.

If you heat a pot of water on the stove, the temperature of the water increases until it reaches 100 °C (212 °F). At 100 °C, water boils, or changes rapidly to a gas called *water vapor*. You can't see water vapor. It's invisible.

Water boils at 100 °C.

What's the Temperature?

▶ Draw a line from each thermometer to the picture that shows the state of water indicated by the temperature on the thermometer.

garden hose

ice cube

boiling water

Now You See It...

Liquid water can change to a gas without boiling. Look at the drawings of a puddle. What changes do you see?

ACTIVE READING As you read these two pages, draw a line under each main idea.

Water can evaporate at temperatures below 100 °C.

Liquid water does not have to boil to become a gas. When you sweat on a hot day, the water on your skin disappears. The liquid water turns into a gas. This is called **evaporation** [ee•vap•uh•RAY•shuhn]. Water can evaporate from other places, such as a puddle.

The sun's heat makes the water in the puddle change to water vapor, which goes into the air.

The puddle gets smaller as the water disappears. Most of the liquid water has changed to a gas.

A gas can change back to a liquid. This is called **condensation** [kahn•duhn•SAY•shuhn]. Water vapor condenses as it cools and loses energy. Water vapor in the air condenses on a cold car window. The outside of a cold soft drink can becomes wet on a hot day. The grass on a cool morning may have dew on it. These are all condensation.

▶ **What happened to water vapor in this girl's warm breath as she breathed on the cold window?**

_____

_____

_____

Sum It Up »

Read the statements. Then draw a line to match each statement with the correct picture.

1 This state of matter does not have a definite size or shape.

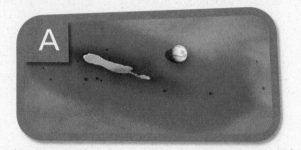

A

2 This state of matter has a definite size and takes the shape of its container.

B

3 During this process, a liquid changes to a gas.

C

4 This state of matter has a definite size and shape.

D

5 During this process, a gas changes to a liquid.

E

Name _____

Vocabulary Review

1 Write four words from the box to complete this word web about the physical properties of matter.

Use the clues to unscramble the blue words. Use the word bank if you need help.

1. **dlois:** Ice is water in this state. _____

2. **sga:** Boiling changes liquid water to this state. _____

3. **iqldui:** At 0°C, ice can change to this state if heat is added. _____

4. **ntaoaevprio:** The water in a puddle changes to a gas through this process. _____

5. **otdoncnaesni:** A gas changes to a liquid through this process _____

condensation   gas   solid   evaporation   liquid

Apply Concepts

2 Make a list of solids, liquids, and gases in your school.

_____

_____

3 Think about what happens to a glass of cold water outside on a hot day. Use the words *evaporation* and *condensation* to describe what happens to the water inside the glass and what happens on the outside of the glass.

_____

_____

_____

4 Which picture shows solid water? Which shows liquid water? Label the pictures.

_____   _____

Take It Home! Share what you have learned about the states of matter with your family. With a family member, name states of matter that are present at mealtime or in places in your home.

SC.3.P.9.1 Describe the changes water undergoes when it changes state through heating and cooling by using familiar scientific terms such as melting, freezing, boiling, evaporation, and condensation. **SC.3.N.1.3** Keep records as appropriate, such as pictorial, written, or simple charts and graphs, of investigations conducted.

Name _____

ESSENTIAL **QUESTION**

How Can the State of Matter Change?

EXPLORE

We use a lot of words to talk about how matter changes state. You can make a mobile to help you remember the terms and what they mean.

Materials

scissors
index cards
string
tape
crayons
glue
clothes hanger

Before You Begin—Preview the Steps

1 Cut out the squares from your book.
CAUTION: Be careful with scissors!

2 Glue each square onto a card. Look at the cards and decide what process is being described. Write your answer on the back of each card.

3 Attach the finished cards to the clothes hanger with string and tape.

4 Display your mobile.

© Houghton Mifflin Harcourt Publishing Company

Set a Purpose

What will you learn from this investigation?

_____

_____

Think About the Procedure

How can you show how matter changes state?

_____

Record Your Data

Name _____

Complete the table by filling in the missing terms or descriptions of changes in state.

Term	Description of Change
melting	
freezing	
	liquid to gas at 100°C
evaporation	
	gas to liquid

Draw Conclusions

Write the terms from the table that describe the change from one state to another state.

gas → liquid → solid

_____

solid → liquid → gas

_____

Claims • Evidence • Reasoning

1. A person wearing eyeglasses leaves an air-conditioned store on a hot day. Her glasses fog up. Write a claim about what happened and give reasons to support your claim.

_____

_____

_____

Claims • Evidence • Reasoning (continued)

2. Give an example of how freezing affects your everyday life during the summer.

_____

_____

3. A recipe for cookies calls for melted butter. In what state must the butter be? What clue word helped you find the answer?

_____

_____

_____

4. What will happen to the volume of liquid water when it boils? Explain your reasoning.

_____

_____

_____

5. A summer rain gets your bike wet. The hot sun comes out. Soon the bike is dry. What happened? Explain your reasoning.

_____

_____

_____

6. Write a question you would like to ask about how matter changes state.

_____

_____

Materials

Name _____

Cut out these boxes along the dotted lines and use them for your mobile.

1. Water cooling at 0 °C

2. Water at 100 °C

3. Pond water drying up on a hot summer day

4. Ice heated at 0 °C

5. Water appearing on the outside of a cold milk carton on a hot summer day

SC.3.N.1.1 Raise questions about the natural world investigate them individually and in teams through free exploration and systematic investigations, and generate appropriate explanations based on those explorations.

S.T.E.M.

ENGINEERING & TECHNOLOGY

Resources on the Road

Machines are made using natural resources. Read about the natural resources used to make a car.

Glass is made from minerals. This glass is coated in plastic. It is hard to recycle.

Seats are cotton and plastic. Cotton comes from plants. Plastic is made from oil. Seats often end up in landfills.

Steel makes up the car's frame. Steel is a mixture of metals and can be recycled.

Tires are made from rubber and metal. Rubber comes from trees. Tires can be recycled.

Why is it important to recycle car parts?

_____

_____

_____

177

Change the Design

The supply of many natural resources is limited. Tell what natural resources make up the bicycle parts.

A bike helmet is a technology that uses cloth and plastic.

cotton and plastic

Pick one part of the bicycle. Tell how you could change the design to use fewer resources.

_____

_____

_____

_____

Design It:
Float Your Boat

When you cross a river, you probably use a bridge. In places where there are no bridges, boats may take cars across rivers. Have you ever wondered how a boat carrying heavy loads stays afloat? Even though the boat and load are very heavy, the boat doesn't sink. That's because it has a special shape that makes it float.

DESIGN PROCESS STEPS

1 Find a Problem
2 Plan & Build
3 Test & Improve
4 Redesign
5 Communicate

What to Do:

1 Roll a small piece of clay into a ball.

2 Fill a bowl with water. Place the clay ball on the water's surface. What happens?

3 Reshape the clay into a small boat. What happens now?

4 How many pennies can this boat support?

5 Keep improving your design to increase the number of pennies your boat can carry. How did you improve your design?

6 Draw and describe your design in your Science Notebook.

Name _____

Vocabulary Review

Use the terms in the box to complete the sentences.

> condensation
> evaporation

1. During _____, water changes from a

   liquid to a gas.

2. During _____, water changes from a

   gas to liquid.

Science Concepts

Fill in the letter of the choice that best answers the question.

3. Jon measures the temperature of water in four containers. The containers have temperatures of 5 °C, 1 °C, 7 °C, and 0 °C. What can Jon infer about the water?

   (A) Two of the containers have solid water in them.

   (B) Only one of the containers has solid water in it.

   (C) Only two of the containers have liquid water in them.

   (D) Only one of the containers has liquid water in it.

4. The temperature of milk in the refrigerator is 5 °C. The temperature of the kitchen is 22 °C. If the milk sits on the kitchen table for 30 minutes, what would its temperature **most likely** be?

   (F) 2 °C   (H) 5 °C

   (G) 12 °C   (I) 30 °C

5. There are two boxes in a classroom. The first box has a drawing of a long, thin, red object on the outside. Inside it are red pencils, red straws, and red markers. The second box has a drawing of a blue circle on the outside. Which objects would **most likely** be found in the second box?

   (A) blue shoes and blue papers

   (B) blue golf balls and red CDs

   (C) blue marbles and blue plates

   (D) blue cups and blue notebooks

6. Yesterday, the temperature of John's pond was –5 °C. Today, the temperature of the pond is 0 °C. Can John ice skate on the pond?

   (F) Yes, the pond is solid ice.

   (G) No, the pond is liquid water.

   (H) No, the pond is starting to condense.

   (I) Yes, the pond is made of water vapor.

7. Onisha wants to sort 20 objects into groups by their color. She wants to record what object was in each group. Which would be the best way to record her sorting?

Ⓐ Draw each of the objects she sorted and staple each drawing into a group.

Ⓑ Make a chart and list the objects into groups the way she sorted them.

Ⓒ Make a bar graph that shows how many objects of each color there are.

Ⓓ List all the objects and put a checkmark by all the blue objects.

8. Look at the objects in the picture below.

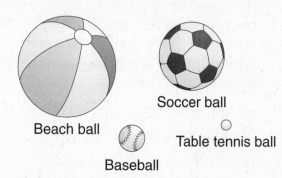

Beach ball

Soccer ball

Baseball

Table tennis ball

Which of the following physical properties is the same for all the balls?

Ⓕ hardness   Ⓗ shape

Ⓖ size   Ⓘ texture

9. Rosa measures the volume of four objects. Rosa places each object into a graduated cylinder of water, one at a time. She measures the starting water level and final water level each time. The table below shows Rosa's results.

	Rock	Marble	Golf ball	Bar magnet
Starting water level (mL)	50	50	50	50
Final water level (mL)	60	57	65	62
Volume of object (mL)				

For which object will Rosa record the largest volume?

Ⓐ rock   Ⓒ marble

Ⓑ golf ball   Ⓓ bar magnet

10. Sam's mom boils water in a pot on the stove. Which of these describes how the state of water changes when the water begins to boil?

Ⓕ gas to liquid

Ⓖ liquid to gas

Ⓗ liquid to solid

Ⓘ solid to liquid

Name _____

11. Beth and T.J. are studying the properties of water. Beth placed a container with 50 mL of water in a freezer. T.J. placed the same kind of container with 25 mL of water in the same freezer. Which will be the same for both containers of water?

   (A) masses of the two containers of frozen water

   (B) time it takes the water in each container to freeze

   (C) temperature at which the water in each container freezes

   (D) amount of space the frozen water in each container takes up

12. Grace has a notebook, two pencils, a red folder, and three books in her backpack. How are all the things in Grace's backpack alike?

   (F) They are all big.

   (G) They are all liquids.

   (H) They are all solids.

   (I) They are the same size.

13. Freezing and melting are opposite processes. Which is the opposite of condensing?

   (A) cooling

   (B) evaporating

   (C) freezing

   (D) melting

14. Min's teacher had the class work in four groups. Each group put a thermometer in a similar cup of water. The groups put their cups near the window in the sunlight. They measured the temperature every 3 minutes for 15 minutes. They wrote the temperatures in the table below.

Time (min)	Group 1	Group 2	Group 3	Group 4
	Temperature (°C)			
0	23	22	23	23
3	23	23	24	23
6	25	24	25	25
9	27	26	25	26
12	28	28	27	28
15	30	28	28	29

What is the **most likely** reason the groups wrote different temperatures in the table?

   (F) The cups did not have the same type of water.

   (G) Some groups wrote down the wrong temperatures.

   (H) The thermometers used by some groups were broken.

   (I) The temperatures were a bit different in each cup of water.

Apply Inquiry and Review the Big Idea

Write the answers to these questions.

15. Ben uses a pan balance to compare the masses of two toy blocks. The image below shows Ben's experiment.

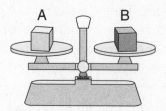

Make a claim about how the masses of the two blocks compare. Cite evidence to support your claim.

_____

_____

_____

16. The thermometer shows the temperature outside.

Make a claim about what will happen to an ice cube if you put it outside. Cite evidence to support your claim and explain how it supports the claim.

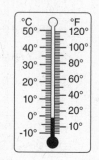

_____

_____

_____

17. The temperature in Jessica's house is 24 °C. The temperature outside is 4 °C. Jessica left a bag of marbles on the table outside. Make a claim about what the temperature of the marbles could be after being outside for 15 minutes. Explain your reasoning.

_____

_____

_____

Forms of Energy

FLORIDA BIG IDEA 10

Forms of Energy

South Florida Symphony conducted by Sebrina María Alfonso performing Beethoven's 9th Symphony, Adrienne Arsht Center, Miami, FL, January 2016.

I Wonder Why

Many people like to go to concerts. Why can everyone in this audience hear the music? *Turn the page to find out.*

Here's Why

The instruments are designed to make sounds. The sound travels through the air to the audience.

Essential Questions and Florida Benchmarks

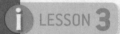

Science Notebook

Before you begin each lesson, write your thoughts about the Essential Question.

SC.3.P.10.1 Identify some basic forms of energy such as light, heat, sound, electrical, and mechanical.
SC.3.P.10.2 Recognize that energy has the ability to cause motion or create change. **SC.3.N.3.1** Recognize that words in science can have different or more specific meanings than their use in everyday language; for example, energy, cell, heat/cold, and evidence.

ESSENTIAL **QUESTION**

What Are Some Forms of Energy?

 Engage Your Brain

Find the answer to the following question in this lesson and record it here.

What makes this toy pop up?

_____

_____

_____

_____

_____

📖 ACTIVE **READING**

Lesson Vocabulary
List the terms. As you learn about each one, make notes in the Interactive Glossary.

_____ _____

_____ _____

_____

Main Idea
The main idea of a section is the most important idea. The main idea may be stated in the first sentence, or it may be stated elsewhere. Active readers look for main ideas by asking themselves, What is this section mostly about?

What's Energy?

"You have lots of energy!" People say that when you run around a lot. So what is energy?

ACTIVE **READING**

As you read this page, draw circles around each paragraph's main idea.

Energy is the ability to make something move or change. If you want to put a book on a shelf, it takes energy to move it up there. What about melting snow? It takes energy to change snow to liquid water.

There are many forms of energy. **Potential energy** is stored energy. **Kinetic energy** is the energy of motion. An object can have potential energy, kinetic energy, or both. An object's **mechanical energy** [muh•KAN•ih•kuhl] is the total of its potential energy and kinetic energy.

188

Potential

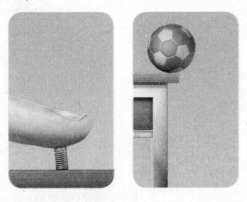

The spring gained potential energy when it was pushed down. The ball gained potential energy when it was lifted onto the table.

Kinetic

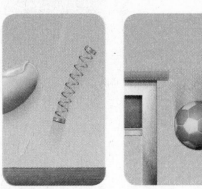

As the spring and the ball move, their potential energy changes to kinetic energy. The mechanical energy of each stays the same. It just changes form.

▶ **Write whether each person or object has potential energy or kinetic energy.**

potential

Where's the Energy?

Energy is all around us every day. It has many different forms.

ACTIVE READING As you read these two pages, underline the names of forms of energy.

Examine Energy

How do you use energy in your home? Write an example for each caption.

Sound Energy

Sound comes from the speakers as music.

_____

_____

Electrical Energy

Electrical energy, or electricity [ee•lek•TRIS•ih•tee], is energy that moves through wires. It makes equipment work.

_____

_____

Heat Energy

Heat from the lights makes the musicians sweat.

_____

_____

Light Energy

Light from the spotlights helps the crowd see the band play.

_____

_____

You use sound energy every day as you talk to your friends and classmates. But think of all the other ways sound energy helps you.

Use Energy

Sound from a whistle gets everyone's attention.

Sound doesn't cook food, but it lets you know when the food is ready.

Sound in the form of music can change your mood!

DO THE MATH

Understand Data Tables

Source of Sound	Sound Level
Lawn Mower	90 dB
Mosquito	10 dB
Conversation	60 dB
Hair Dryer	90 dB
Ringing Phone	80 dB
Chainsaw	110 dB

Units called decibels (dB) are used to measure the loudness of sounds. Sounds louder than 85 dB can damage your ears.

1. Which two sources are the safest for your hearing?

_____

2. Which source makes sound that is 25 dB above the safe level?

_____

3. Which two sources give off the same amount of sound?

_____

4. Which source gives off 30 less decibels than the chainsaw?

_____

Sum It Up »

Use information in the summary to complete the graphic organizer.

Energy is the ability to move or change something. Potential energy is stored energy. Kinetic energy is the energy of movement. An object may have both kinetic and potential energy. The total of these is its mechanical energy. Any form of energy can change into another form.

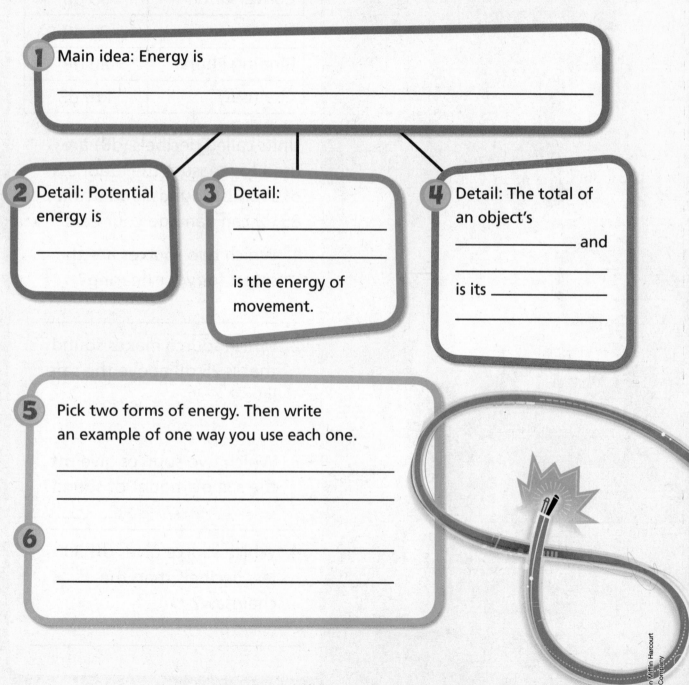

1 Main idea: Energy is

_____

2 Detail: Potential energy is

_____

3 Detail:

_____
_____

is the energy of movement.

4 Detail: The total of an object's

_____ and
_____

is its _____

_____

5 Pick two forms of energy. Then write an example of one way you use each one.

_____

_____

6 _____

_____

© Houghton Mifflin Harcourt Publishing Company

Name _____

Vocabulary Review

1 Unscramble each word and write it in the boxes.

1. **G E E R N Y**
This lesson is about different forms of
____.

2. **L A P N E T O T I**
Stored energy

3. **L L E E R C T I A C**
A form of energy that moves through wires

4. **I T I N E C K**
The energy of motion

Write the letters in the circles here.
Unscramble them to form two more words.

_ _ _ _ _ _ _ _ _ _ _ _ _ _

9. The energy that is a total of # 2 and #4

10. A form of energy you can see that comes from the sun

5. **A T H E**
A form of energy you can feel from the sun

6. **N U O D S**
A form of energy that might wake you up in the morning

7. **E V M O**
Energy is the ability to make something do this.

8. **G N C A H E**
Energy is also the ability to make something do this.

Apply Concepts

2 Write the form of energy each object takes in.

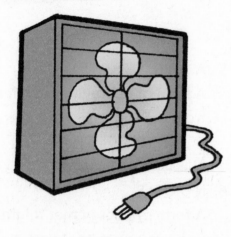

_____

4 Write the form of energy each object produces.

_____

3

_____

5

_____

Take It Home! _See ScienceSaurus®_ for more information about energy.

SC.3.N.1.1 Raise questions about the natural world, investigate them individually and in teams through free exploration and systematic investigations, and generate appropriate explanations based on those explorations.

S.T.E.M.

ENGINEERING & TECHNOLOGY

Telephone Timeline

Suppose you get some great news. You want to share it with your friend who lives many miles away. What can you do? You can send your friend a text or call him or her on the phone. Sharing news was not always this easy. Phones did not always exist. Use the timeline below to see how phones have changed over the years.

To use the first phones, callers needed an operator to connect them to the person they were calling. These phones were connected by wires. Voices were not always very clear.

In the early 1900s, callers could dial the number they wanted or use an operator. The receiver was still connected to the phone base with a cord. Voices were clearer on these phones.

Cordless phones were introduced in the 1980s. They had separate bases and could be used around the house. The receivers had buttons used for calling. Some phones had adjustable volumes to help make voices clearer.

Are the phones you use at home similar to those on this page? What are some of the differences between your phones at home and those on this page?

_____

_____

_____

S.T.E.M. continued

Predict an Upgrade

Today, phones can do many things. Draw in the box your idea for a phone of the future. Describe it on the lines provided. Be sure to list what new features your phone has and why.

Design It:

Make a Musical Instrument

There are many different types of instruments that make music. Many instruments make music with strings. Some instruments use wind, and some are tapped or hit to make music. Most instruments have ways to change the pitch of the music they make.

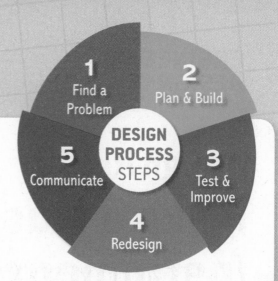

DESIGN PROCESS STEPS

1 Find a Problem
2 Plan & Build
3 Test & Improve
4 Redesign
5 Communicate

What to Do:

1. Draw a picture of your instrument design.

2. What materials will you select? How will your instrument make music? How will you make your instrument change pitch?

3. Use selected classroom materials to assemble your instrument.

4. Try your instrument to see if it works the way you planned.

5. Use a sound recorder to collect, record, and analyze how your instrument sounds.

6. Keep a record of your work in your Science Notebook.

SC.3.P.10.1 Identify some basic forms of energy such as light, heat, sound, electrical, and mechanical. SC.3.N.1.1 Raise questions about the natural world, investigate them individually and in teams through free exploration and systematic investigations, and generate appropriate explanations based on those explorations...

Learn About ...
Benjamin Franklin

Benjamin Franklin was born in January 1706. He moved from Boston to Philadelphia in 1723. Franklin worked as a printer and made newspapers. Later, he became a scientist and an inventor. He discovered that lightning is a form of electricity. In 1752, Franklin flew a kite in a rainstorm. A wire on the kite attracted electricity in the cloud. The electricity went down the string to a metal key. Scientists still study electricity today.

Fun Fact

Did you know that Franklin once used a kite to pull him while swimming?

Read the timeline below. Use what you read about Benjamin Franklin to fill in each blank box.

1706 Franklin is born in Boston, Massachusetts.

1750 Franklin invents the lightning rod to protect buildings from lightning.

Think About It!

In what ways does electricity make our lives easier?

_____

_____

_____

_____

_____

SC.3.P.10.3 Demonstrate that light travels in a straight line until it strikes an object or travels from one medium to another. **SC.3.P.10.4** Demonstrate that light can be reflected, refracted, and absorbed.

LESSON 2

ESSENTIAL QUESTION

How Does Light Move?

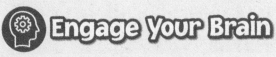 Engage Your Brain

Find the answer to the following question in this lesson and record it here.

What's wrong with the writing on the ambulance? It's backwards! Why?

_____

_____

_____

_____

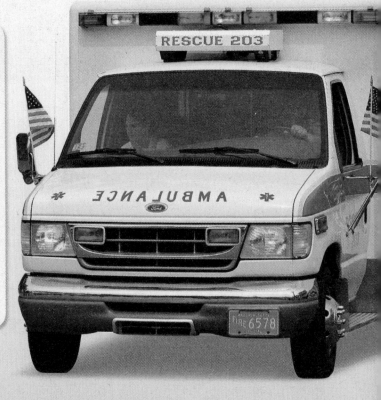

📖 ACTIVE READING

Lesson Vocabulary
List the terms. As you learn about each, make notes in the Interactive Glossary.

_____

_____

_____

_____

Cause and Effect
Signal words show connections between ideas. Words signaling a cause include because and if. Words signaling an effect include so and thus. Active readers remember what they read because they are alert to signal words that identify causes and effects.

203

A Lighted Path

Light is all around us. Light's movement allows us to see. How?

ACTIVE **READING** As you read these two pages, draw a circle around the clue word that signals a cause.

Light moves in straight lines. In the picture at the top of this page, the flashlight beam is a straight line. The beam does not bend or curve. Look at the picture below. The top of the light beam is a straight line, and the bottom of the light beam is a straight line. The whole light beam is straight.

The light is below the boy's face. The shadow of his nose is above his nose.

What happens when light hits an object? It cannot keep going straight.

Objects can absorb light. **Absorb** means to take in. The marshmallow and the stick block light. They either absorb or bounce back all of the light that hits them. No light goes through.

The marshmallow and stick have a shadow. A **shadow** is the dark area behind an object that has blocked light. The shadow has a shape that is similar to the object. That's because light travels in straight lines.

The light in the tent is blocked by the kids' bodies. They absorb most of the light that hits them. You can see the shadows on the side of the tent.

▶ One of these lights is on. It is making a shadow behind the block. Draw a circle around the light that is on.

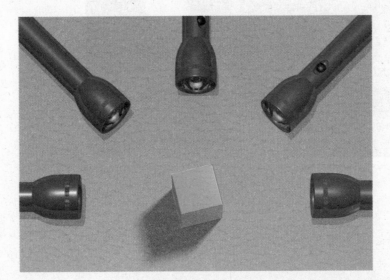

Seeing Double

Not all objects absorb light. Some objects bounce light back in the opposite direction.

ACTIVE READING As you read these two pages, find and underline three facts about reflecting.

A surface can **reflect**, or bounce back, light. Smooth glass, metal, and water reflect well. Picture a calm lake. The image on the lake is formed by light reflecting off its surface.

The beam of the flashlight below is shining downward. It traveled in a straight line until it hit an object that reflected it. The light bounced back up when it reflected.

Did you ever notice that things look backward in a mirror? Words are hard to read if you reflect them in a mirror because they're reversed. A reflected image is always reversed.

No Fishing!

▶ Use a hand mirror to read this sign. What does it say?

_____

▶ Draw the reflection of the canoe in the water.

Bend It!

Glass and water can reflect light. They can also bend light.

ACTIVE READING As you read these two pages, underline the definition of *refract*.

> Refraction quacks me up!

refraction

Light can **refract**, or bend, when it moves from one clear material to another. When the beam hits the water in the tank, it refracts.

► Fill in the cause. Then circle the place in the photo where refraction occurs.

Cause

_____

_____

Effect

An object may appear broken

It's easy to see where light is refracted. Just look for the break! What makes the duck look broken? Light reflects from the duck above water and underwater. Light from the duck's top half goes straight to your eyes. Light from its bottom half goes through water first. The light refracts as it leaves the water. This makes the duck's belly and legs look separated from the top half of its body!

Reflection and Refraction

These binoculars reflect light so that it is directed to your eyes.

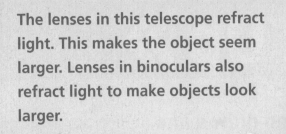

The lenses in this telescope refract light. This makes the object seem larger. Lenses in binoculars also refract light to make objects look larger.

If light didn't reflect, you'd never be able to see yourself in a mirror. If light didn't refract, there would be no telescopes, cameras, microscopes, or eyeglasses.

All of these items use lenses. Their lenses are made to refract. Items such as these depend on refracting lenses to work.

DO THE **MATH**

Multiply Whole Numbers

Tom watches a robin. It appears about three inches in size. He then watches it through binoculars.
The robin now appears to be nine inches in size. How many times as large did the robin look through the binoculars?

Sum It Up »

Finish the summary statements. Then draw a line to match each statement with the correct image.

1 When light passes through a clear material, it bends, or _____ .

2 Some objects take in, or _____ light.

3 Behind an object that absorbs light, you will see a dark spot called a _____ .

4 When light hits a shiny surface, it bounces back, or _____ .

5 Light travels in a _____ path.

Name _____

Vocabulary Review

1 Draw a line from each term to its definition or description.

1. absorb*

2. binoculars

3. lens

4. reflect*

5. refract*

6. reversed

7. shadow*

8. straight

A. Its purpose is to refract light.

B. An area that light cannot reach

C. To bounce back in the opposite direction

D. Bend, as light does when it moves from air to water

E. Marshmallows reflect and ____ light when it hits them.

F. Objects in mirrors look like this

G. The kind of path light travels in

H. Uses lenses to reflect and refract light

* Key Lesson Vocabulary

Apply Concepts

2 Draw a circle around the item that reflects light. Draw a square around the item that refracts light. Draw a triangle around the item that absorbs light.

3 Label each diagram.

_____ _____

4 In the box, draw the path the light would take from the flashlight.

Take It Home! With your family, go through your home, looking for two things that reflect light, two things that refract light, and two things that absorb light.

SC.3.P.10.3 Demonstrate that light travels in a straight line until it strikes an object or travels from one medium to another. SC.3.P.10.4 Demonstrate that light can be reflected, refracted, and absorbed. SC.3.N.1.2 Compare the observations made by different groups using the same tools and seek reasons to explain the differences across groups. SC.3.N.1.7 Explain that empirical evidence is information...that is used to help validate explanations of natural phenomena.

ⓘ INQUIRY LESSON 3

Name _____

ESSENTIAL QUESTION
What Surfaces Reflect Light Best?

Materials
flashlight
various objects

EXPLORE

Light travels in a straight line. If something gets in its way, the light will be absorbed, reflected, or refracted. In this activity, you will determine whether certain objects reflect light. Recording accurate observations *reflects* well on you, by the way!

Before You Begin—Preview the Steps

1. Look at the objects provided by your teacher. Examine the surface of each one. Then make a hypothesis about the kind of surface that will reflect light best.

2. Based on your hypothesis, choose two objects that you predict will reflect light well and two that you predict will reflect light poorly.

3. Turn off the lights. Shine the flashlight on one of the objects. Observe whether it reflects light onto the wall. Record your observation.

4. Repeat Step 3 for the other objects. Record your observations.

Set a Purpose

What will you learn in this investigation?

_____

_____

_____

State Your Hypothesis

Write your hypothesis, or testable statement.

_____

_____

Think About the Procedure

What is the tested variable?

_____

_____

Why should you use the same light source with each object?

_____

_____

_____

Name _____

Record Your Data

Record your setup and results in the boxes. Use one box for each object tested.

Draw Conclusions

What did you observe as you tested each object?

_____

_____

_____

Claims • Evidence • Reasoning

1. Write a claim about the way shiny and dull objects respond to light.

   _____

   _____

2. Cite evidence from the activity that supports your claim and explain why the evidence supports the claim.

   _____

   _____

   _____

   _____

3. Can you think of a real-life situation that could be used as evidence of the same claim?

   _____

   _____

   _____

4. Why do you think some objects did not reflect light onto the wall? Explain your reasoning.

   _____

   _____

5. What similarities, if any, did you observe in the way the objects responded to the light?

   _____

   _____

6. Think of other questions you would like to ask about things that reflect light.

   _____

   _____

Name _____

Vocabulary Review

Check the box to show whether each statement is about a potential energy or kinetic energy or both.

Potential	Kinetic	
☐	☐	1. stored energy
☐	☐	2. type of energy
☐	☐	3. energy of motion

Science Concepts

Fill in the letter of the choice that best answers the question.

4. There are different types of energy. Which item is an example of electrical energy?

   (A)  (C)

   (B) 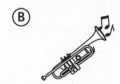 (D)

5. Kendall feels tired after riding his bicycle. He uses a blender to make a healthy shake. Which types of energy are used and output by the blender?

   (F) electrical; heat and light

   (G) electrical; potential and heat

   (H) electrical; kinetic and sound

   (I) mechanical; sound and potential

6. Dan turns on an electric fan, a flashlight, a lamp, and the television. Which one gives off both light and sound energy?

   (A) electric fan   (C) lamp

   (B) flashlight   (D) television

7. Students are enjoying a field trip. They see activities that involve different types of energy. Edie is looking at the archery exhibit.

Which explanation tells what happens when the girl lets go of the bow?

(F) Potential energy becomes kinetic energy.

(G) Kinetic energy becomes potential energy.

(H) Mechanical energy becomes light energy.

(I) Mechanical energy becomes electrical energy.

8. A ball falls off a shelf. What is the evidence that it has energy as it falls?

(A) The ball is round, and all round objects have energy.

(B) The ball is moving, and things that are moving have energy.

(C) The ball is very heavy, and energy is what gives objects weight.

(D) The ball is falling toward Earth, and energy pulls objects toward Earth.

9. Midori's mom heats bread in an electric toaster oven. As it heats, the coils inside the oven glow. The oven beeps when the bread is done. The oven uses different types of energy. Study the chart below.

A	heat
B	light
C	electrical
D	sound

Which types of energy are present during this process?

(F) A only

(G) A and B only

(H) A, B, and C only

(I) A, B, C, and D

10. Mia pointed a flashlight straight ahead. The light traveled forward. Then it suddenly traveled straight back at Mia. Which of the following objects did the light **most** likely strike?

(A) brick wall

(B) large mirror

(C) clear glass window

(D) frosted glass window

11. Damon has a watch with a solar panel on it. The solar panel stores energy from sunlight. Which of the following **most** likely happens when sunlight strikes the solar panel?

(F) Sunlight is reflected.

(G) Sunlight is refracted.

(H) Sunlight is absorbed.

(I) Sunlight is transmitted.

Name _____

12. Drew and Amy each took a glass and placed water in it. Drew used faucet water, and Amy used water from a fountain. They wrapped their glasses with white paper and placed them under a light. The temperatures after 20 minutes are shown below.

Cup	Temperature (°C)
Drew's cup	30
Amy's cup	25

What might explain the difference in Drew's and Amy's temperatures?

(A) Drew's water evaporated, and Amy's did not.

(B) Drew used a different color of paper than Amy did.

(C) Drew's starting temperature was different from Amy's.

(D) Drew's water was placed under a light, and Amy's water was in the shade.

13. Raul sits at his desk to study. On his desk are a drinking glass, lamp, fan, and books. Based on the way the term *energy* is used in science, which of these is true?

(F) The books have kinetic energy.

(G) The glass has potential energy.

(H) The lamp has sound energy.

(I) The fan has light energy.

14. Rylee and Ming each hold an end of a bent hollow tube. They shine a light through the end, but cannot see it at the other end of the tube. Which tells why they cannot see the light?

(A) The light that they are using is too dim, so it cannot travel that far.

(B) Light travels in a straight line. The tube is bent, so it absorbs the light.

(C) The tube is too dark. If they try a lighter tube, the light will show up.

(D) The openings are not large enough to allow the light to enter and exit.

15. Blake is standing in a pond looking at fish. From above the water, they look large. From under the water, they look smaller. What happens to light as it travels from the water to the air?

(F) It stops.   (H) It reflects.

(G) It bends.   (I) It is absorbed.

16. Sammy places jeans into an electric clothes dryer and pushes the power button. Which explanation tells what happens in the dryer?

(A) Electrical energy changes into heat energy.

(B) Electrical energy changes into potential energy.

(C) Potential energy changes into electrical energy.

(D) Mechanical energy changes into electrical energy.

Apply Inquiry and Review the Big Idea

Write the answers to these questions.

17. A light meter measures how much light is given off. Javier and Lucas measure light from a flashlight. They both place their meters in the beam of light. Javier's meter registers more light. Why might Javier's meter have registered more light than Lucas's meter? Explain your reasoning.

_____

_____

_____

18. A skier is perched atop a hill. Suddenly she pushes off and glides downhill. Make a claim about the potential and kinetic energy of the skier at the top of the hill and when she is moving down the hill.

_____

_____

_____

19. Maria entered a dark room. She shined a flashlight on a chair. She claimed that the chair absorbed the light rather than reflecting it. What could she observe as evidence that supports her claim? Explain how the evidence supports her claim.

_____

_____

_____

© Houghton Mifflin Harcourt Publishing Company

Heat Sources

FLORIDA **BIG IDEA 11**

Energy Transfer and Transformations

Lightning strikes in Florida.

I Wonder Why

Lightning is bright. But lightning also sometimes starts fires. Why? *Turn the page to find out.*

Here's Why

Lightning gives off light, but it also gives off heat. The temperature of a lightning bolt can be hotter than the surface of the sun! No wonder it can set things on fire.

Essential Questions and Florida Benchmarks

 **Science Notebook**

Before you begin each lesson, write your thoughts about the Essential Question.

SC.3.P.11.1 Investigate, observe, and explain that things that give off light often also give off heat. **SC.3.P.11.2** Investigate, observe, and explain that heat is produced when one object rubs against another, such as rubbing one's hands together. **SC.3.N.3.1** Recognize that words in science can have different or more specific meanings than their use in everyday language; for example, energy, cell, heat/cold, and evidence.

LESSON 1

ESSENTIAL **QUESTION**

What Are Some Heat Sources?

🧠 Engage Your Brain

Find the answer to the following question in this lesson and record it here.

The brakes on a car rub against the wheels to stop the car. But why are this car's brakes bright orange?

_____

_____

_____

📖 ACTIVE **READING**

Lesson Vocabulary

List the terms. As you learn about each one, make notes in the Interactive Glossary.

_____

_____

Main Idea

The main idea of a section is the most important idea. The main idea may be stated in the first sentence, or it may be stated elsewhere. Active readers look for main ideas by asking themselves, What is this section mostly about?

Sharing the Warmth

Here are two common words: heat and temperature. You hear them every day. But what do they really mean?

ACTIVE **READING** As you read these two pages, circle the clue word or phrase that signals a detail such as an example or an added fact.

Scientists use words very carefully. Some common words have special meanings in science. For example, when you use the word *heat*, you might mean how warm something is. In science, **heat** is energy that moves from warmer objects to cooler objects.

The temperature of the water in these hot springs is higher than the temperature of the monkeys. Heat flows from the warmer water to the monkeys. The monkeys feel warmer.

Temperature is the measure of how hot or cold something is. Temperature can be measured in degrees. Water with a temperature of 32 °C (90 °F) is hotter than water with a temperature of 12 °C (54 °F).

Remember, heat is energy. Heat always moves from an object with a higher temperature to one with a lower temperature.

Heat Can Move

▶ In each picture, heat will flow from one object to another. Draw an arrow to show which way it will flow.

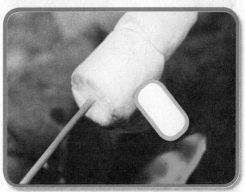

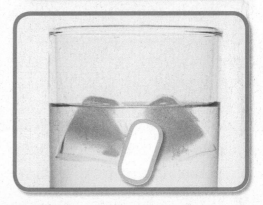

The red part of the metal horseshoe has a very high temperature. Heat moved from the fire into the red part of the horseshoe.

Turn Up the Heat

Heat moves from something warmer to something cooler. You rely on that every day. How? Here is just one way.

Would you like to eat nothing but raw food? Ugh! For things to cook, they must gain heat energy.

Heat moves from the blue flames to the pot. Then it moves from the pot to the stew. The heat cooks the stew.

① This oven is used to bake food. Heat moves from the oven to the air inside the oven. Then it moves from the hot air to the food. The heat from the oven baked these cookies!

② Some things slow the movement of heat. The woman in the picture is using oven mitts. The mitts slow the movement of heat, so she does not get burned.

DO THE **MATH**

Read a Table

1. What foods are cooked at 145 °F?

_____

2. Which food needs to be cooked at a higher temperature, eggs or chicken?

_____

3. What food is cooked at 160 °F?

_____

Safe Food Cooking Temperatures

Type of Food	Cooking Temperature
Eggs	160 °F
Salmon	145 °F
Beef	145 °F
Chicken	165 °F

Hot Light

Old-fashioned light bulbs give off heat. Some newer kinds give off more light and less heat.

It's not unusual to see something glowing red and giving off heat. That's what the lava is doing in this picture.

Have you ever touched a light bulb that had been on for a while? The heat may have surprised you!

ACTIVE READING As you read these two pages, draw a star next to what you consider to be the most important sentence, and be ready to explain why.

You've learned that heat is energy. But remember, light is a form of energy, too. Heat and light often occur together. Many things that give off light also often give off heat.

The light bulb is used for its light, but it also gives off heat. The coil inside a toaster gives off heat. That's how the bread gets toasted. But the coil also gives off an orange-red light. When something gives off both light and heat, we often want to use just one or the other.

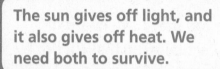

The sun gives off light, and it also gives off heat. We need both to survive.

▶ Heat and Light Sources

How many things in your house give off light and heat? List some of them here.

_____

_____

_____

_____

The charcoal is giving off orange light. It also gives off the heat that cooks the meat.

The light from a candle's flame can let us see in a dark room. The heat from the flame melts the wax.

Burn Rubber

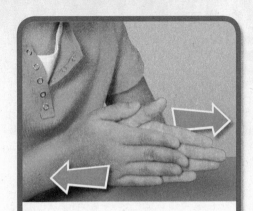

If you're ever out in the cold without gloves, rub your hands together. The heat you produce will warm your hands!

Q: Can you make a fire by rubbing two sticks together?

A: Yes, if one of them is a match!

That's an old joke, so you may have heard it before. However, you actually can make a fire by rubbing two sticks together. You have to move them quickly, and you must have something nearby to burn. But it can be done. Where do you think the heat comes from?

ACTIVE READING As you read these two pages, draw circles around two words or phrases that are key to understanding the main idea.

The tires are rubbing against the road as they spin. They're spinning very quickly and producing a lot of heat. They're getting so hot that they're burning. That's where the smoke is coming from.

When two things rub against each other, there is *friction* [FRIK•shuhn] where they touch. Friction produces heat. The faster and harder the two things rub, the more heat is produced.

Where Is Heat Produced?

In each photo, two things are rubbing together to produce heat. Draw a circle around the point where the heat is being produced. Then write a caption for each picture.

_____

_____

_____

_____

_____

_____

_____

_____

Sum It Up >>

Write the correct word in the blank.

1 Things that give off
_____ often
give off heat as well.

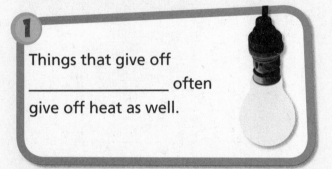

2 _____ is
measured in degrees.

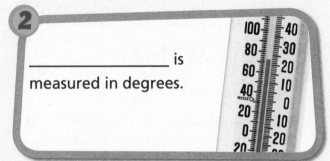

Complete the graphic organizer.

Heat

can be produced by (3) _____
two things (4) _____.

is a form of (5) _____.

always flows from a
(6) _____ object to a
(7) _____ object.

Name _____

Vocabulary Review

1 **Use the clues to help unscramble each word. Write the unscrambled word in the boxes.**

Something with a higher temperature is

E T H O T R

☐ ☐ ☐ ☐ ⊙ ☐

Something that is hot may do this.

W L G O

⊙ ☐ ☐ ☐

The measure of how hot or cold something is

M T E E R P U T A R

☐ ☐ ☐ ☐ ☐ ⊙ ☐ ☐ ☐ ☐ ☐

Friction from spinning race car tires might cause this.

M K S O E

⊙ ☐ ☐ ⊙ ☐

This produces heat when two things rub together.

I T R N F I C O

☐ ⊙ ☐ ☐ ☐ ☐ ☐ ☐

Something with a very low temperature is this.

O C D L

☐ ☐ ☐ ⊙ ☐

Unscramble the letters in the circles to form a word that is related to this lesson.

☐ ☐ ☐ ☐ ☐ ☐ ☐ ☐

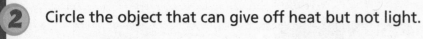

Apply Concepts

2 Circle the object that can give off heat but not light.

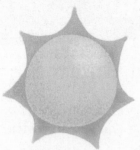

sun
_____

candle
_____

hot chocolate
_____

3 Name two things you sometimes do to prevent heat from being transferred.

_____

_____

_____

_____

4 Name two things that give off both light and heat.

_____

5 Name one way that you use heat.

_____

 **Take It Home!** See *ScienceSaurus®* for more information about heat energy.

SC.3.P.11.2 Investigate, observe, and explain that heat is produced when one object rubs against another . . . SC.3.N.1.1 Raise questions about the natural world . . . generate appropriate explanations . . . SC.3.N.1.2 Compare the observations made by different groups . . . SC.3.N.1.7 Explain that empirical evidence is information...that is used to help validate explanations of natural phenomena.

INQUIRY
LESSON 2

Name _____

ESSENTIAL **QUESTION**

Where Can Heat Come From?

EXPLORE

Warm up those hands! In this activity, you and your classmates will explore a way to produce heat. As you do each step, record how warm each material feels.

Before You Begin—Preview the Steps

(1) Rub your hands quickly together for 30 seconds. Record your observations.

(2) Rub the two cloths together for 30 seconds. Record your observations.

(3) Rub the paper against the wood for 30 seconds. Record your observations.

(4) Put 5 drops of soapy water between the paper and the wood. Rub for 30 seconds. Record your observations.

Materials

1 sheet of paper
2 pieces of cloth
1 block of wood
soapy water

Set a Purpose

What do you think is the purpose of this investigation?

_____

_____

_____

State Your Hypothesis

Why are you using different items to rub together?

_____

_____

_____

Name _____

Record Your Data

Record your results in the table below.

Setup	Hot?	Observations
hands rubbed against each other		
clothes rubbed against each other		
paper rubbed against **wood** with **nothing** between them		
paper rubbed against **wood** with **soapy water** between them		

Draw Conclusions

Compare your results with the other groups. Why might they have different results?

_____

_____

Claims • Evidence • Reasoning

1. Write a claim about the relationship between rubbing objects together and heat. Cite evidence that supports your claim. Explain your reasoning.

_____

_____

_____

Claims • Evidence • Reasoning (continued)

2. If two parts of a machine rub together, what could you do to keep them from getting as hot? Use observations to explain your reasoning.

_____

_____

_____

3. How would you plan an investigation to find possible materials to reduce friction?

_____

_____

_____

_____

4. Ramp 1 has a smooth surface. Ramp 2 has a sandpaper surface. Will the book on either ramp move? Explain your reasoning.

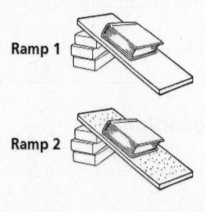

Ramp 1

Ramp 2

_____

_____

_____

_____

SC.3.P.11.1 Investigate, observe, and explain that things that give off light often also give off heat. SC.3.N.1.1 Raise questions about the natural world...and generate appropriate explanations based on those explorations.

Ask a Volcanologist

Q. What does a volcanologist do?

A. A volcanologist is a person who studies volcanoes. We can warn people when a volcano will erupt. People will have time to get to safety.

Q. How do you stay safe when working around lava?

A. I wear special clothes, gloves, and boots to protect me from the heat. I wear a gas mask to protect me from volcanic gases.

Q. How do you know that lava is very hot?

A. Lava is very hot! You know that lava is hot because it gives off heat and light. It may glow bright orange, yellow, or red.

Now It's Your Turn!

▶ What question would you ask a volcanologist?

_____

_____

_____

_____

Be a Volcanologist

Volcanologists can tell lava's temperature by the color it glows.

Match each temperature below to the lava flowing from the volcano. Write the temperature in the correct location.

1100°C   bright orange

850°C   bright red

650°C   dark red

200°C   black

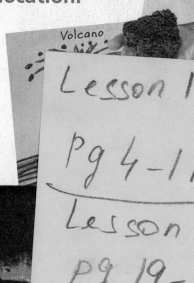

Volcano

Lesson 1

Pg 4 - 11

Lesson 3
pg 19 - 27

Name _____

Vocabulary Review

Use the terms in the box to complete the sentences.

| temperature |
| heat |

1. When you measure how hot or cold something is,

   you measure its _____ in degrees.

2. _____ moves from warmer objects

   to cooler objects.

Science Concepts

Fill in the letter of the choice that best answers the question.

3. Sandra's mother is boiling water on a stove. In which picture does the arrow show the direction that heat moves to make the water boil?

   Ⓐ

   Ⓑ

   Ⓒ

   Ⓓ

4. Hiroto wants to warm a pot of soup on a stove. He will put the pot onto one of the stove's heat elements and turn it on.

   Heat elements

   Which heat element does Hiroto know is very hot, without touching them?

   Ⓕ the biggest one

   Ⓖ the smallest one

   Ⓗ the one that glows red

   Ⓘ the one that looks dark

5. Lucas is having a birthday party. He has ice cream, balloons, and a cake with candles.

Which of the objects shown in the picture produces the most heat?

Ⓐ cake

Ⓑ candles

Ⓒ balloon

Ⓓ ice cream

6. Nolan picks up a book from his desk and hands it to his teacher. His teacher sets the book down and slides it across a table. Which action produces the most heat?

Ⓕ sliding the book across a table

Ⓖ handing the book to his teacher

Ⓗ setting the book down on a table

Ⓘ picking the book up from his desk

7. Marvin and Byron both hold a thermometer close to a light bulb. After 2 minutes, they record their measurement. Marvin records 67 °C. Byron records 65 °C. Why might they have different results?

Ⓐ The light bulb is not the same temperature on all sides.

Ⓑ Marvin held his thermometer closer to the bulb than Byron did.

Ⓒ One of the thermometers was not working correctly.

Ⓓ Marvin read the Fahrenheit temperature instead of the Celsius temperature.

8. Jamal is toasting marshmallows over a campfire.

Which of the following signs shows that the fire is probably hot?

Ⓕ It has sticks in it.

Ⓖ It has bright flames.

Ⓗ It has ashes around it.

Ⓘ It has sand under the logs.

Name _____

9. A mover pushes a box up a ramp into a truck.

Which two things become warmer when the man pushes the box?

Ⓐ box and air

Ⓑ ramp and box

Ⓒ man and truck

Ⓓ truck and ramp

10. Energy can change form. Which picture shows electrical energy changing into heat energy?

11. Jason is sanding a board with sandpaper. He puts a piece of sandpaper around a block of wood and sands the board. Which of the following terms has a specific meaning in science that could relate to Jason's activity?

Ⓐ experiment

Ⓑ evidence

Ⓒ heat

Ⓓ sanding

12. Matthew's class investigates friction between smooth items and rough items. They find that rough items produce more friction. Which of the following items would create the most heat if rubbed together for 20 seconds?

Ⓕ

Plastic containers

Ⓖ

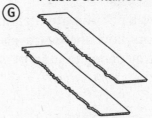

Rough cardboard

Ⓗ

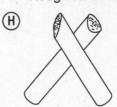

Chalk

Ⓘ

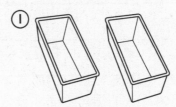

Baking pans

Apply Inquiry and Review the Big Idea

Write the answer to this question.

13. Jenna and Tanner want to decrease the friction between a wooden block and a ramp. They cover the ramp with two different materials and slide the block down the ramp on each material. They record their results in the table.

Ramp covering	How object moved	
	Faster	Slower
Plastic tablecloth	X	
Cloth tablecloth		X

Make a claim about which ramp-covering material created the least amount of friction with the block. Cite evidence to support your claim and explain your reasoning.

_____

_____

_____

_____

_____

14. The picture shows a pot of water heating on a stovetop.
Make a claim about how energy travels to the water in the pot and what happens to the water. Use evidence to support your claim and explain how it supports your claim.

_____

_____

_____

Plants and the Environment

An orchard grows in Florida.

FLORIDA BIG IDEA 14

Organization and Development of Living Organisms

I Wonder Why

Like animals, plants are living things. But most plants can't eat food. Why do they survive? *Turn the page to find out.*

Here's Why

Plants can make their own food. They use sunlight, air, and water to make food. This process takes place in their leaves.

Essential Questions and Florida Benchmarks

 Science Notebook

Before you begin each lesson, write your thoughts about the Essential Question.

(bg) ©George Tiedemann/GT Images/Corbis; (inset) ©George Tiedemann/GT Images/Corbis; (border) ©NDisc/Age Fotostock

© Houghton Mifflin Harcourt Publishing Company

SC.3.L.14.1 Describe structures in plants and their roles in food production, support, water and nutrient transport, and reproduction. **SC.3.N.3.2** Recognize that scientists use models to help understand and explain how things work. **SC.3.N.3.3** Recognize that all models are approximations of natural phenomena; as such, they do not perfectly account for all observations.

LESSON **1**

ESSENTIAL **QUESTION**

What Are Some Plant Structures?

 Engage Your Brain

Find the answer to the following question in this lesson and record it here.

What do the roots at the bottom of this plant do for the plant?

_____

_____

 ACTIVE **READING**

Lesson Vocabulary
List the terms. As you learn about each one, make notes in the Interactive Glossary.

_____ _____

_____ _____

_____

Sequence
Many of the ideas in this lesson are connected by a sequence, or order, that describes the steps in a process. Active readers stay focused on sequence when they mark the transition from one step in a process to another.

249

Get to the Bottom of It

Plants come in many shapes and sizes. Did you know that an important part of most plants is hidden underground?

ACTIVE READING As you read this page, circle lesson vocabulary words when they are defined.

Plants are made up of different parts. Each part has a function that helps the plant grow and survive.

The part of the carrot plant that we eat is its root. Roots hold plants in the ground. Roots also take in, or absorb [uhb•SOHRB], water and nutrients from the soil. **Nutrients** [NOO•tree•uhntz] are materials that living things such as plants need to grow.

Some roots are long and can reach water deep under the ground. Some roots have many small, hairy branches that spread out just under the soil to get water from a large area. Water and nutrients move from the roots to other parts of the plant.

A plant's roots absorb water and nutrients from the soil.

carrot

pansy

grass

Roots Come in All Sizes and Shapes

Look at the pictures of roots on this page. Fill in the table to compare and contrast the roots. How are they alike? How are they different?

Roots		
	Alike	**Different**
Carrot		
Pansy		
Grass		

Reach for the Sky

oak tree

What happens to water and nutrients after they enter the roots? How do they get to the rest of the plant?

Water and nutrients move from the roots to the stem. The stem is the part of the plant that helps the plant stand tall and strong. It holds up the part of the plant that is above ground. A stem also carries water and nutrients from the roots to other parts of the plant.

The woody stems of most trees are big and thick. The stems of flowers are often soft and thin. Some plants have one main stem, but others have many.

A plant's stem carries water and nutrients from the roots to the rest of the plant.

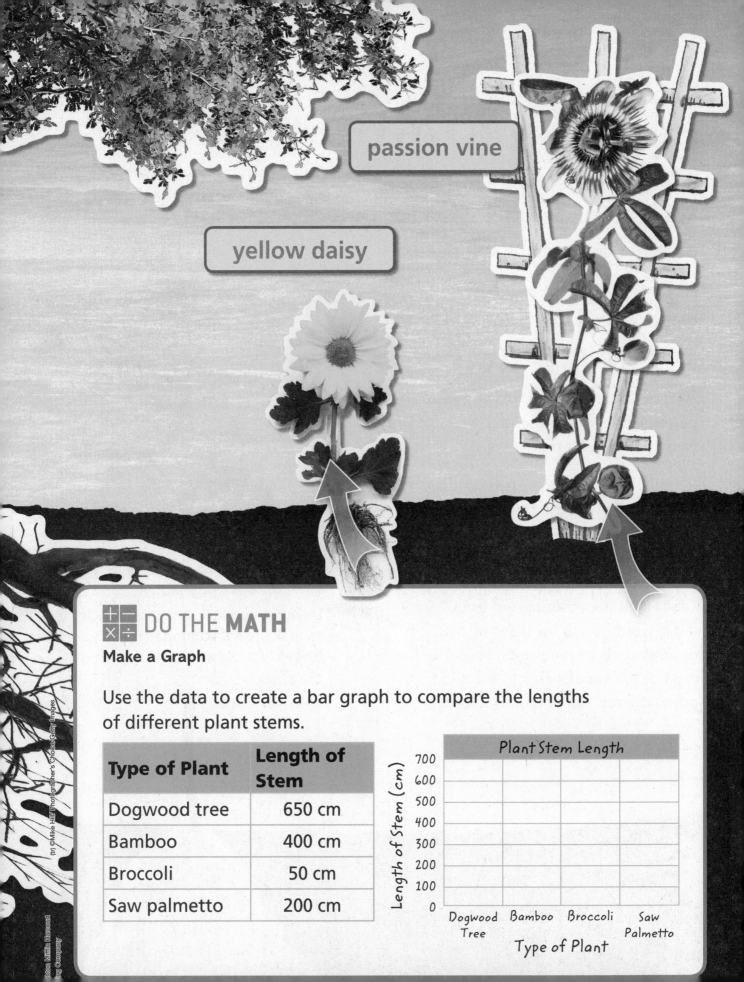

passion vine

yellow daisy

DO THE **MATH**

Make a Graph

Use the data to create a bar graph to compare the lengths of different plant stems.

Type of Plant	Length of Stem
Dogwood tree	650 cm
Bamboo	400 cm
Broccoli	50 cm
Saw palmetto	200 cm

Plant Stem Length

Length of Stem (cm)

700
600
500
400
300
200
100
0

Dogwood Tree · Bamboo · Broccoli · Saw Palmetto

Type of Plant

Plant Food!

Water and nutrients keep a plant healthy. But a plant still needs food to survive. Luckily, a plant doesn't need to go anywhere to get its food!

ACTIVE **READING** As you read these pages, draw one line under a cause. Draw two lines under an effect.

Unlike animals, most plants can make their own food. This important process takes place in leaves.

Leaves use water, air, and light energy from the sun to make food. The food is then transported from the leaves through the plant's stems to other parts of the plant. Plants use most of this food energy to live and grow. The rest of the food is stored.

sunflower

Leaves use water, air, and sunlight to make food. Food made in leaves is transported to the rest of the plant.

palm tree

Leaves are many different sizes and shapes. Look at the picture of the sunflower plant. Its leaves are big and wide. Big, wide leaves can catch more sunlight. This helps the plant make more food.

bush

Show the Flow

Draw a plant growing in soil. Draw different-colored arrows to show how water, nutrients, and food move in different directions through the plant.

The Cycle of Life

The tallest tree in the world was once small enough to fit in your hand. Like you, plants start out small and grow bigger.

ACTIVE READING As you read this page, write numbers next to the appropriate sentences to show the order of steps in the reproduction of an apple tree.

The blossoms on apple trees and other plants are called flowers. A **flower** is the plant part that helps some plants reproduce [ree•pruh•DOOS]. When living things **reproduce**, they make new living things like themselves.

First, flowers grow into fruit. After the fruit ripens, it falls to the ground. The fruit contains seeds. A **seed** has a small plant inside of it. A seed also has food for the small plant.

Then sunlight, soil, water, and air help the seeds sprout into seedlings and grow. The seedlings grow into adult plants. The life cycle continues as the adult plants produce more flowers and seeds.

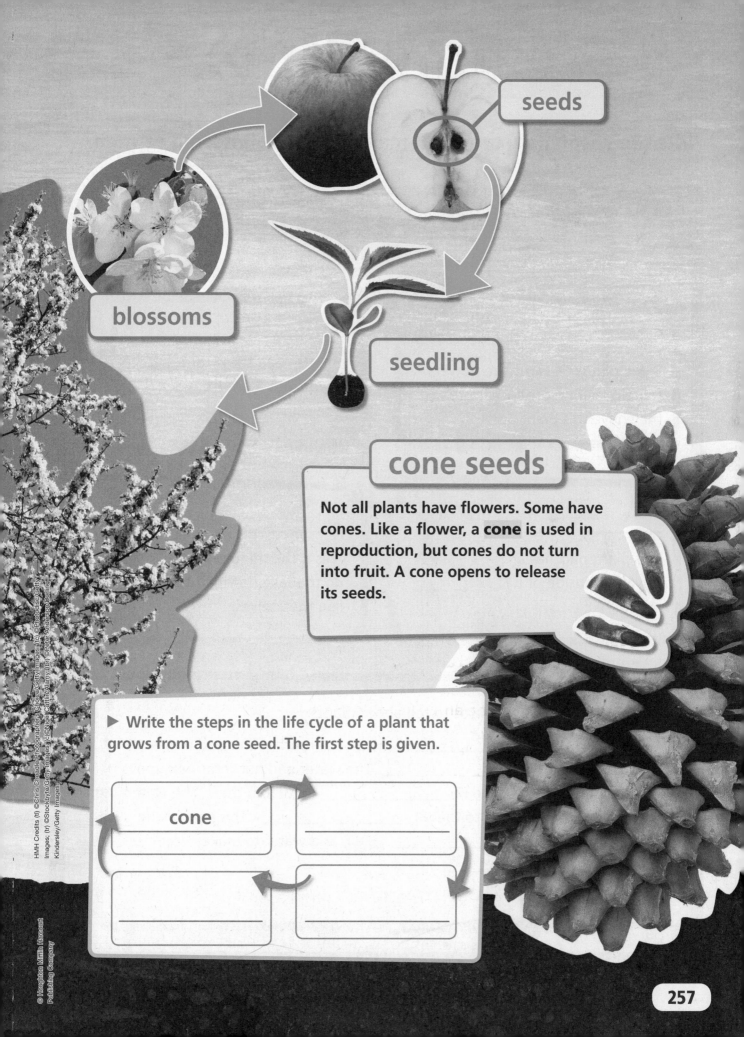

seeds

blossoms

seedling

cone seeds

Not all plants have flowers. Some have cones. Like a flower, a **cone** is used in reproduction, but cones do not turn into fruit. A cone opens to release its seeds.

▶ Write the steps in the life cycle of a plant that grows from a cone seed. The first step is given.

cone _____ _____

_____ _____

Sum It Up »

Write the vocabulary term that matches each photo and caption.

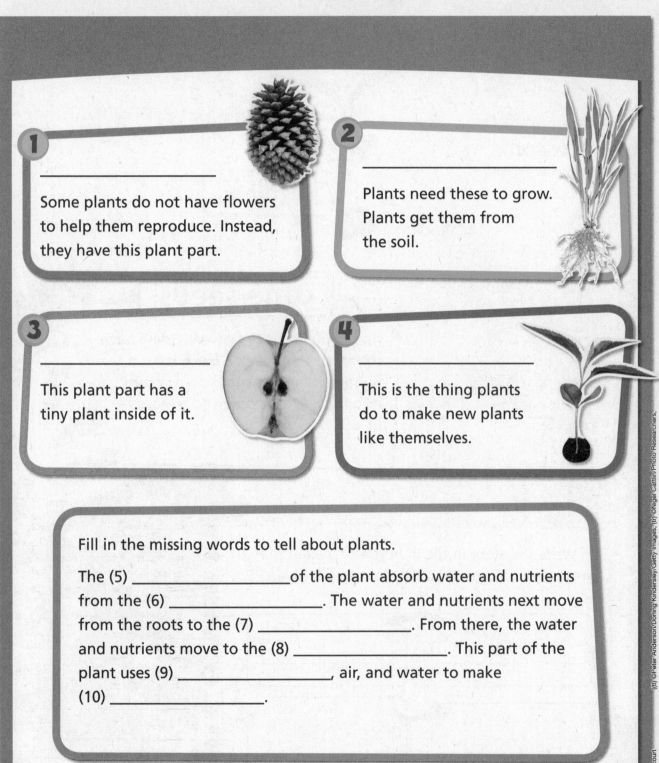

1 _____

Some plants do not have flowers to help them reproduce. Instead, they have this plant part.

2 _____

Plants need these to grow. Plants get them from the soil.

3 _____

This plant part has a tiny plant inside of it.

4 _____

This is the thing plants do to make new plants like themselves.

Fill in the missing words to tell about plants.

The (5) _____ of the plant absorb water and nutrients from the (6) _____. The water and nutrients next move from the roots to the (7) _____. From there, the water and nutrients move to the (8) _____. This part of the plant uses (9) _____, air, and water to make (10) _____.

Name _____

Vocabulary Review

1 Use the words in the box to identify the parts of a plant. Tell one function of each part.

| roots | stem | leaf | flower* | *Key Lesson Vocabulary |

Apply Concepts

2 Draw the life cycle of a peach tree. The first stage is already done.

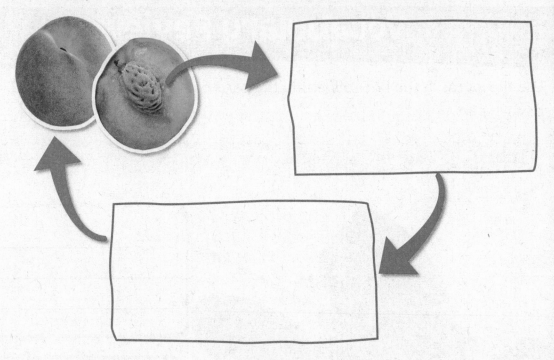

Find two different types of plants near your school.

3 How are these plants different?

_____

4 How are these plants similar?

_____

_____

5 Which parts of the two plants can you see?

_____

See *ScienceSaurus®* for more information about plants.

SC.3.L.14.1 Describe structures in plants and their roles in food production, support, water and nutrient transport, and reproduction.

PEOPLE **IN SCIENCE**

1 Rosa Ortiz is a botanist. She studies plants.

2 Ortiz studies a family of plants called the moonseed family.

3 Moonseed is a woody vine. It has poisonous parts.

5 Things to Know About

Rosa Ortiz

4 Ortiz travels to many places to study moonseed.

5 The roots of some types of moonseed have been used as medicine.

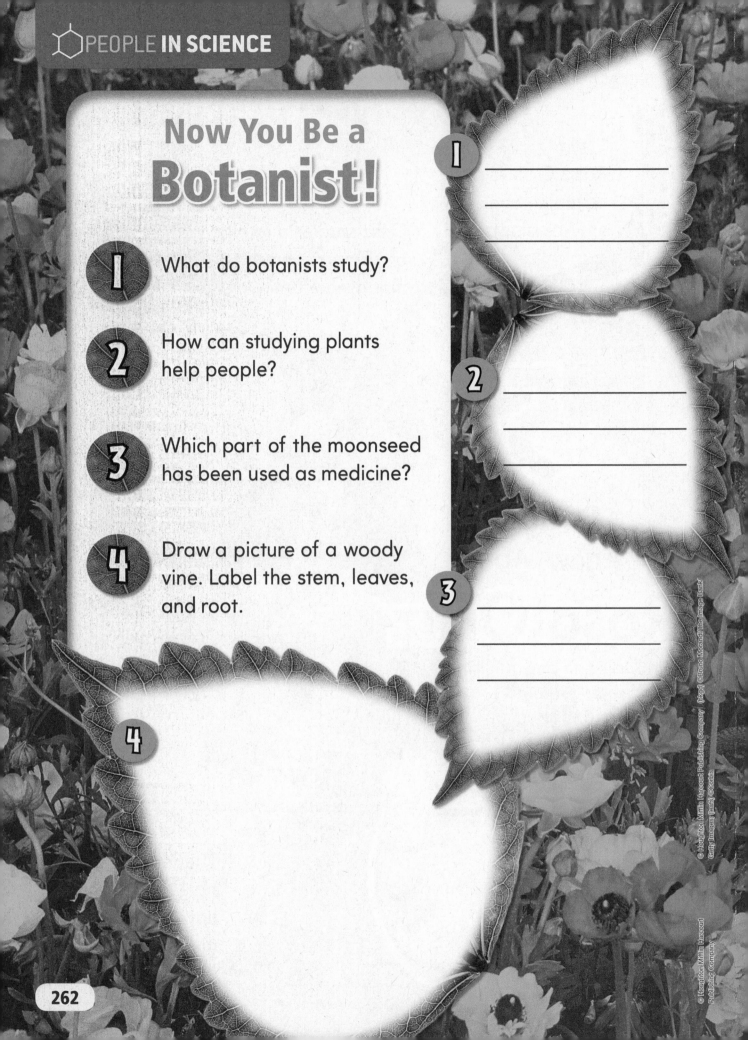

Now You Be a Botanist!

1 What do botanists study?

2 How can studying plants help people?

3 Which part of the moonseed has been used as medicine?

4 Draw a picture of a woody vine. Label the stem, leaves, and root.

1 _____

2 _____

3 _____

4

SC.3.L.14.1 Describe structures in plants... SC.3.L.14.2 Investigate and describe how plants respond to stimuli... SC.3.N.1.3 Keep records as appropriate... SC.3.N.1.4 Recognize the importance of communication among scientists. SC.3.N.1.5 Recognize that scientists question, discuss, and check each other's evidence and explanations. SC.3.N.1.6 Infer based on observations.

i INQUIRY LESSON **2**

Name _____

ESSENTIAL QUESTION

How Do Plants Respond to Light?

Materials

bean seedling

water

1 shoebox with a 5-centimeter hole in one end

EXPLORE

You know that plants need sunlight to make food. In this activity, you will explore how plants respond to light.

Before You Begin—Preview the Steps

① Get your bean seedling and box from your teacher.

② Place your seedling in the box. Put the lid on the box.

③ Place the box on a sunny windowsill. The opening in each group's box should face a different direction.

④ Observe your seedling each day for 5 days. Record your observations. Water your seedling as needed.

© Houghton Mifflin Harcourt Publishing Company

Set a Purpose

In this investigation, you will share your results with other groups. Why do you think scientists share their results?

_____

_____

_____

Think About the Procedure

Why does each group face the opening in its shoebox in a different direction?

_____

_____

_____

Predict what will happen to the seedlings.

_____

_____

_____

Name _____

Record Your Data

In the space below, draw how the seedlings responded to light.

Starting the Investigation	After Day 3	After Day 5

Draw Conclusions

What did you observe about the seedlings? Infer why the seedlings responded as they did.

_____

_____

_____

_____

Claims • Evidence • Reasoning

1. Compare your observations with those of other groups. Did all groups have the same results? Why or why not?

_____

_____

_____

2. Write a claim about plants based on your observations.

_____

_____

3. Cite evidence that supports your claim.

_____

_____

4. Explain why your evidence supports your claim.

_____

_____

_____

_____

5. Plants respond to temperature as well as light. How could you design an experiment to find out how temperature affects plants?

_____

_____

_____

_____

SC.3.L.14.2 Investigate and describe how plants respond to stimuli (heat, light, gravity), such as the way plant stems grow toward light and their roots grow downward in response to gravity. **SC.3.N.1.6** Infer based on observation.

ESSENTIAL **QUESTION**

How Do Plants Respond to Their Environment?

Engage Your Brain

Find the answer to the following question in this lesson and record it here.

This tree fell over and then began growing upward again. Why?

_____

_____

_____

 ACTIVE **READING**

Lesson Vocabulary
List the terms. As you learn about each one, makes notes in the Interactive Glossary.

_____

_____

Main Idea and Details
Detail sentences give information about a topic. The information may be examples, features, characteristics, or facts. Active readers stay focused on the topic when they ask, What fact or information does this sentence add to the topic?

Plants and Light

What happens when you go from a dark room into a bright room? You blink! Blinking is a response to light. Plants respond to light, too.

ACTIVE READING As you read these two pages, draw two lines under each main idea.

Hi. My name is Maria. I like learning about plants. One day, I put my plant in a dark room with one window. A week later, it looked like this! The plant began growing toward the light.

Growing toward light is one way that plants respond to their environment. The **environment** is all the living and nonliving things in a place. Growing toward light helps plants make more food.

Morning glory flowers open in the morning sun and last only one day.

By afternoon, the flowers close up and die.

Flowering plants respond to light in more than one way. The flowers of some plants open during the day and close at night. Other plants have flowers that open at night and close during the day. The bright yellow flowers of the sunflower plant face the sun throughout the day. The flowers move from east to west, following the sun as it crosses the sky.

What Will the Plant Do?

Look at the picture of the plant on the opposite page. Imagine that you turned the plant around so that it was growing away from the light. Explain and draw what would happen to the plant.

_____

_____

_____

The Heat Is On!

What happens when it gets very warm out? You sweat! Sweating is a response to the rising temperature. Plants respond to rising temperatures, too.

ACTIVE **READING** As you read these pages, circle the sentences that explain how plants respond to a change in temperature.

In the winter, the branches of a tree in my grandmother's yard were bare. In spring, the temperature changed, and the weather got warmer. The tree was covered with buds!

This tree gets buds in the spring.

Hyacinth bulbs must go through a period of cooler weather before they will grow again in the warmer temperatures of springtime.

Leaf budding is one way that plants respond to heat. The buds come out when the temperature warms. The buds change into leaves.

How else do plants respond to temperature changes? Temperature affects when seeds germinate. **Germinate** [JER•muh•nayt] means that the seeds start to grow.

You might notice that when the temperature is warmer in spring, seedlings begin to grow. For example, acorns begin to grow into oak trees.

Some plants will not release their seeds unless it is burning hot! Some pinecones only open and release their seeds after a forest fire.

What's the Effect?

Fill in the chart below to show details about plants and heat.

> **Plants respond to temperature.**

Some cones release their seeds in response to fire.

Cold Snap

What happens when it's really cold outside? Your teeth chatter! Plants respond to cold weather, too.

In late fall, the oranges on our orange tree were ready to pick. Before we could pick them, the weather got really cold. There was a freeze. The fruit was ruined!

Weather below 0 °C, or a *freeze*, can harm a plant. Sometimes the freeze happens when the plant is flowering. The flowers die. The plant will not produce fruit. Sometimes the freeze happens when the fruit is on the tree. As Maria said, the fruit is ruined!

A freeze damaged these trees and fruit.

Cold weather has not damaged these oranges. They are ready to pick.

There are ways to keep plants safe from freezes. People can spray the fruit with water. Ice forms over the fruit and protects it from the cold!

➕✖️➗ DO THE MATH

Interpret a Graph

The graph shows the number of ripe oranges picked from Maria's tree for five years. Study the graph and then answer the questions.

Number of Oranges on Maria's Tree

Year	Oranges
2006	🍊🍊🍊🍊🍊🍊🍊
2007	🍊🍊🍊🍊
2008	🍊🍊
2009	🍊🍊🍊🍊
2010	🍊🍊🍊🍊🍊🍊🍊🍊🍊🍊

Key: Each 🍊 = 10 oranges

1. How many oranges were picked each year?

_____

_____

_____

_____

2. In which years do you think a freeze occurred? Why?

_____

_____

_____

_____

Up or Down?

What happens when you jump? Gravity pulls you back. Plants respond to gravity, too.

ACTIVE READING As you read this page, find and underline details about a plant responding to gravity.

Gravity pulls things toward Earth's center. A plant's roots respond to gravity by growing mostly downward. A plant's stem responds in the opposite way. The stem grows upward, away from the pull of gravity. Even when a plant gets tipped on its side, the plant's stem will slowly start to grow upward again.

Stems grow up.

Roots grow down.

Growing against the pull of gravity gave this tree a bend in its trunk.

I know that gravity makes plant roots grow downward and stems grow upward. So what would happen if I turned a bean plant on its side?

The stem of this bean plant grows upward, away from gravity.

On its side, the bean plant's stem continues to grow opposite the pull of gravity.

▶ Predict what the plant will do if the pot is turned upright again.

_____

_____

_____

▶ Draw what the plant will look like after a few weeks.

Sum It Up »

Complete the graphic organizer using details from the summary below.

Plants respond to their environment. They grow toward light. Plant leaves bud and seeds germinate when the temperature is right. Their roots and stems grow in certain directions in response to the pull of gravity.

1 Detail: _____
_____
_____

Main Idea: Plants respond to their environment.

2 Detail: _____
_____
_____

3 Detail: _____
_____
_____

Name _____

Vocabulary Review

1 Use the words in the box to complete each sentence.

1. Some pine cones open only when _____ is very high.

2. _____ is another name for forming flowers or leaves.

3. _____ pulls things towards Earth's center.

4. All of the living and nonliving things around a living thing is the

   _____.

5. To _____ is to begin to grow.

budding   environment*   germinate*   gravity   temperature

*Key Lesson Vocabulary

Apply Concepts

2 Draw an arrow from the cause to the effect.

3 In the image above, what is the cone doing in response to heat?

_____

4 Draw arrows to show which direction roots and stems will grow in response to gravity.

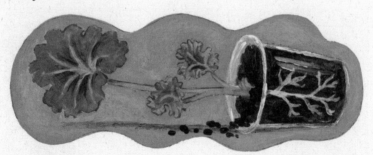

5 What is happening in the picture?

_____

_____

_____

_____

Take It Home!

Share what you have learned about plant responses with your family. Explain how a plant responds to light, temperature, and gravity.

SC.3.N.3.2 Recognize that scientists use models to help understand and explain how things work.

S.T.E.M.

ENGINEERING & TECHNOLOGY

Firefighting Tools:
Controlling Forest Fires

Fires play an important role in many forest ecosystems. But large forest fires can damage habitats and homes. Firefighters use special tools to help control forest fires.

Special aircraft dump water or chemicals that stop fires.

Some tools protect firefighters. This coat is made from material resistant to fire.

Tools like the Pulaski help clear trees and brush. This creates a firebreak. *Firebreaks* stop fires from moving into certain areas.

This GPS (Global Positioning System) tool gets information from satellites. It tells firefighters the location of fires.

How can tools help firefighters protect an important habitat?

_____

_____

Solve a Problem

Firefighters need tools to help them stay safe. Other people need safety tools, too. Think of a tool that can help people stay safe. Draw the tool. Tell how it works.

A shovel helps clear underbrush.

_____

_____

_____

_____

_____

_____

_____

_____

How does your tool help people stay safe?

_____

_____

_____

_____

_____

ENGINEERING DESIGN CHALLENGE

Design It:
Draw a Safari Backpack

What sort of things would you need to explore an ecosystem? Design a backpack to find out.

S.T.E.M. continued

DESIGN PROCESS STEPS

1 Find a Problem
2 Plan & Build
3 Test & Improve
4 Redesign
5 Communicate

What to Do:

1. Choose an ecosystem you'd like to explore. Learn more about it.

2. What would you study or collect in that ecosystem?

3. What tools would you need?

4. Draw a picture of a safari backpack that contains the tools you'll need to study the ecosystem.

5. Tell how you would test your backpack design.

6. Keep a record of your work in your Science Notebook.

Image credit text needed

Name _____

Vocabulary Review

Use the terms in the box to complete the sentences.

| seeds |
| reproduce |
| environment |

1. Plants respond to their _____

   by growing toward light.

2. Flowers help a plant _____,

   or make more plants like itself.

3. Fruits and cones both contain _____.

Science Concepts

Fill in the letter of the choice that best answers the question.

4. Look at the diagram of the plant below.

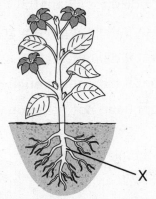

   What is a function of the part of the plant labeled X?

   Ⓐ to hold the plant in the ground

   Ⓑ to make food for the plant

   Ⓒ to help the plant reproduce

   Ⓓ to transport water to the leaves

5. Martin puts a seedling plant in a glass of water. He knows the plant will absorb the water. In what order will the water travel through the parts of the plant?

   Ⓕ leaves, roots, stem

   Ⓖ roots, leaves, stem

   Ⓗ roots, stem, leaves

   Ⓘ stem, leaves, roots

6. Kiara makes a model of an apple tree. She includes leaves, roots, and stems. Which part is missing?

   Ⓐ seeds   Ⓒ cones

   Ⓑ flowers   Ⓓ acorns

7. A class was divided into small groups to do experiments with plants and light. Each group used the same kind of plants. The chart below shows the data from two of the groups.

Plant number	Location	Bending toward light?
Group 1		
1	outside	no
2	inside by window	yes
3	inside in dark corner	yes
Group 2		
1	outside	no
2	inside by window	yes
3	inside in dark closet	no

Which explains why one of the inside plants did **not** bend toward the light?

(F) Some plants do not need light.

(G) Inside plants usually do not bend toward light.

(H) The plant in the corner did not get enough fresh air.

(I) If a plant does not sense light, it won't bend toward that light.

8. Joella places Plant A and Plant B in a sunny spot. They are the same type of plant and put in the same type of soil. She waters Plant A every other day and Plant B only once a week. After two weeks, the plants look like this.

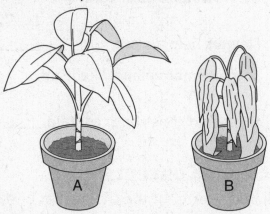

Which statement **best** explains what Joella can conclude about Plant B?

(A) Plant B did not get any food.

(B) Plant B did not get any nutrients.

(C) Plant B did not get enough water.

(D) Plant B did not get enough sunlight.

9. Study the plant parts in the picture.

What will you find inside both of these plant parts?

(F) seeds   (H) tiny leaves

(G) flowers   (I) tiny plants

Name _____

10. Katrina observes the plant part shown here with a hand lens.

    Which statement **best** describes what Katrina can write in her science notebook about this plant part?

    Ⓐ It is the part that gets water from the ground.

    Ⓑ It is the part of the plant in which food is made.

    Ⓒ It is the part of the plant that will bloom into a flower.

    Ⓓ It contains a small plant that can grow into a larger plant.

11. Food is made in the leaves of plants. Which answer **best** explains the pathway of food through the plant?

    Ⓕ leaves to stems to roots

    Ⓖ leaves to flowers to roots

    Ⓗ leaves to roots to flowers

    Ⓘ leaves to flowers to stems

12. Florida is known for its year-round mild weather, but one spring the temperatures did not rise above 21 °C. The table below shows the temperatures at which different plants bud.

Plant	Budding temperatures (°C)
1	13 to 15
2	17 to 20
3	23 to 25
4	23 to 26
5	24 to 26

    Which of the plants were able to bud?

    Ⓐ plants 1 and 2   Ⓒ plants 3 and 4

    Ⓑ plants 2 and 3   Ⓓ plants 4 and 5

13. Carlos has drawn this picture of a plant he is studying. He labels one part of the plant and marks it A.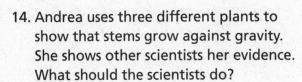

    What caption should Carlos write next to the letter A?

    Ⓕ Makes food

    Ⓖ Absorbs water

    Ⓗ Anchors the plant

    Ⓘ Carries nutrients

14. Andrea uses three different plants to show that stems grow against gravity. She shows other scientists her evidence. What should the scientists do?

    Ⓐ check her evidence

    Ⓑ give her an award

    Ⓒ tell her that her conclusion is wrong

    Ⓓ tell her she did not use enough plants

15. Mohammad draws a diagram of a flowering plant in his science notebook. He draws a line next to a leaf on the plant. Which of the following would be the **best** label for this part of the plant?

    Ⓕ Makes food

    Ⓖ Absorbs water

    Ⓗ Attracts insects

    Ⓘ Transports water

16. Some wheat plants need to go through a period of cold temperatures to grow into adult plants. When would be the **best** time to plant these wheat seeds?

    Ⓐ spring   Ⓒ fall

    Ⓑ summer   Ⓓ winter

Apply Inquiry and Review the Big Idea

Write the answers to these questions.

17. Denise tested a plant to see if it would grow toward light. She placed a seedling next to a sunny window. What evidence will she most likely observe after a week that supports her claim? Explain how the evidence supports her claim.

_____

_____

_____

Make a claim about how Jorge's results will compare to Denise's results. Explain your reasoning.

_____

_____

18. Some tree blossoms are hardy. That means they can survive a bad frost. Other tree blossoms are not hardy. They are easily hurt by frost. The table below shows the hardiness of different tree blossoms.

Tree blossom	Hardiness
grapefruit	somewhat hardy
lemon	not hardy
lime	not hardy
orange	somewhat hardy
mandarin	hardy

Make a claim about which two tree blossoms would be **least** likely to survive a frost. Cite evidence to support your claim. Explain your reasoning.

_____

_____

Classifying
Plants
and Animals

FLORIDA **BIG IDEA** 15

Diversity and Evolution of Living Organisms

The Everglades, Florida

I Wonder Why

The Roseate Spoonbill is one of the animals that lives in the Everglades. How might its name give you a clue about its habitat? *Turn the page to find out.*

Here's Why

The name Spoonbill tells us that it has a bill, like a duck. It used its bill to scoop food out of the water.

Essential Questions
and Florida Benchmarks

Science Notebook

Before you begin each lesson, write your thoughts about the Essential Question.

SC.3.L.15.2 Classify flowering and non-flowering plants into major groups such as those that produce seeds, or those like ferns and mosses that produce spores, according to their physical characteristics.

LESSON 1

ESSENTIAL **QUESTION**

How Can We Classify Plants?

 Engage Your Brain

Find the answer to the following question in this lesson and record it here.

The sticky parts of the sundew plant catch insects. How is this sundew like an orchid?

_____

_____

 ACTIVE **READING**

Lesson Vocabulary

List each term. As you learn about each one, make notes in the Interactive Glossary.

_____

_____

_____

Visual Aids

A photo adds information to the text that appears on the page with it. Active readers pause their reading to review the photos and decide how the information in them adds to what is provided in the text.

Sorting Plants

There are so many plants! How can you classify, or group, them? Let's find out.

ACTIVE READING As you read these two pages, draw circles around two words that are key to understanding the main idea.

One way to classify plants is to group them by their type. For example, think about how all trees are the same or how all shrubs are the same.

Another way to classify plants is to look at their parts. You can group plants that have similar leaves, stems, or roots.

vine

Kinds of Plants

There are many kinds of plants. Vines, trees, and shrubs are three kinds of plants. Vines have long, thin stems. Trees are woody plants that grow tall. Trees have one main stem. Shrubs are similar to trees, but smaller and with many stems.

tree

shrub

pine needle

Plant Parts

One plant part you can use to classify a plant is its leaves. Look at their shape, color, and size. Pine needles are long, thin, and green. Maple leaves have many points. They can be many different shades of green. Palm leaves are very large and fan-shaped or feather-like.

palm leaf

maple leaf

How to Group?

How else can you classify plants?

_____

Draw two plants that you can classify this way.

Blooming!

Roses, tulips, daisies—how are they the same? Read on to find out.

ACTIVE **READING** As you read these two pages, draw circles around the names of flowering plants.

Plants that make flowers are classified as **flowering plants**. Flowering plants are the largest plant group. They are found in deserts, rain forests, and even under water. The flowers of plants have many sizes, colors, and shapes. Let's look at some!

▶ Circle yes or no to classify these plants.

Does it make flowers?

yes   no

Does it make seeds?

yes   no

Orchids are the largest family of flowering plants.

The corpse flower is the largest flower of all. It can weigh more than 20 pounds!

Some hibiscus plants grow flowers all year long.

Seeds

Flowers may look pretty, but they have a job to do. They make fruits with seeds. Oranges and strawberries are examples of fruits with seeds. Each seed has a new plant inside it.

Some magnolia trees grow large, pink flowers.

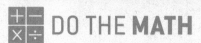 **DO THE MATH**

Use Patterns

Write the number of petals on each flower. Then draw a flower that could complete each pattern.

Cones!

Not all plants make flowers. Some plants make seeds in other ways.

ACTIVE READING As you read this page, draw a star next to what you think is the most important sentence. Be ready to explain why.

   Non-flowering plants are plants that do not make flowers. Even though they do not make flowers, many non-flowering plants make seeds. Pine trees are non-flowering plants. Their seeds develop inside cones. Take a look at other plants that make seeds in cones.

▶ Circle yes or no to classify these plants.

Does it make flowers?   yes   no

Does it make seeds?   yes   no

Sequoia [si•KWOY•uh] trees grow very tall, but they make small cones!

Joint firs grow in dry places. They make small red cones.

Plant Riddle

Read the riddle, then write the answer.

I am very tall.

I grow small cones compared to my size.

What am I?

_____

These eastern cape cycads [SY•kadz] make cones like the ones shown above.

Even More!

Plants with flowers make seeds. Plants with cones make seeds.

Do all plants make seeds? Find out.

ACTIVE **READING** As you read these two pages, draw a line from each picture to one sentence that describes it.

Mosses and ferns are also non-flowering plants. Mosses are small, soft plants. They often grow together in groups. Ferns are larger plants with leaves called fronds.

Mosses and ferns do not make flowers, cones, or seeds. They make spores. Like seeds, **spores** are plant parts that can grow into new plants.

Mosses can grow on rocks and trees. Mosses do not grow tall. This "green carpet" is actually made up of many tiny moss plants.

Ferns have leaves called fronds. Each leaf has smaller leaflets that branch off from the stem.

Spores

Spores are released from the stalks of this moss. In ferns, spores form in small groups on the underside of the fronds. Each group contains hundreds of spores.

moss

fern

This staghorn fern grows on trees.

▶ Read each statement. Circle T if the statement is true and F if it is false.

1. Spores are seeds.   T   F
2. Spores are found in cones.   T   F
3. Mosses do not make flowers.   T   F
4. Ferns make flowers.   T   F
5. Mosses do not make seeds.   T   F

Sum It Up »

The idea web below summarizes the lesson. Give two examples of each type of plant described below.

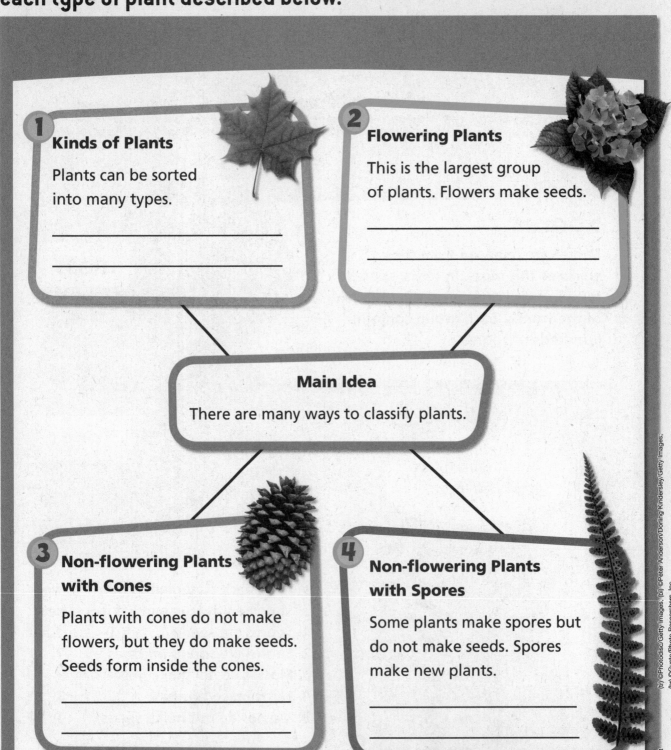

1 Kinds of Plants

Plants can be sorted into many types.

_____

_____

2 Flowering Plants

This is the largest group of plants. Flowers make seeds.

_____

_____

Main Idea

There are many ways to classify plants.

3 Non-flowering Plants with Cones

Plants with cones do not make flowers, but they do make seeds. Seeds form inside the cones.

_____

_____

4 Non-flowering Plants with Spores

Some plants make spores but do not make seeds. Spores make new plants.

_____

_____

Name _____

Vocabulary Review

1 Read the clues. Unscramble the letters to complete the clue.

1. When you group something, you
   _ _ _ _ _ _ _ _ _ _ it.

   y s l i c f s a

   _____

2. Some plants make tiny _ _ _ _ _ _ _
   instead of seeds.

   p r o s s e

   _____

3. _ _ _ _ _ _ grow on some non-flowering
   plants and hold new seeds inside them.

   c s e o n

   _____

4. Plants with _ _ _ _ _ _ _ _ , such as roses
   and daisies, are the largest group of plants.

   r o w e l f s

   _____

5. _ _ _ _ _ plants are small non-flowering
   plants that grow from spores.

   s m o s

   _____

6. _ _ _ _ _ _ have special leaves called
   fronds.

   f r e s n

Apply Concepts

2 Write the letter of the correct description under each picture.

a. I grow seeds and make flowers. Who am I?

b. I grow seeds, but they form in cones. Who am I?

c. I don't grow flowers or seeds. Who am I?

_____   _____   _____

3 Suppose scientists find a new kind of plant in a rain forest. What are three questions they might ask to help them classify the plant?

_____

_____

_____

_____

_____

_____

Take It Home!

See *ScienceSaurus*® for more information about plants.

SC.3.L.15.1 Classify animals into major groups (mammals, birds, reptiles, amphibians, fish, arthropods, vertebrates and invertebrates, those having live births and those which lay eggs) according to their physical characteristics and behaviors. **SC.3.N.3.2** Recognize that scientists use models to help understand and explain how things work.

ESSENTIAL QUESTION

How Can We Classify Vertebrates?

Engage Your Brain

Find the answer to the following question in this lesson and record it here.

How would you classify this animal?

_____

_____

_____

_____

ACTIVE READING

Lesson Vocabulary

List each term. As you learn about each one, make notes in the Interactive Glossary.

_____

_____

_____

_____

Signal Words: Comparison

Signal words show connections between ideas. Words that signal comparisons, or similarities, include *like*, *alike*, *same as*, *similar to*, and *resembles*. Active readers remember what they read because they are alert to signal words that identify comparisons.

Have a Backbone!

Some boas live in thick forests. Their backbones let them curl up and stretch out!

What do you have in common with fish, alligators, frogs, birds, and seals? Why, it's your backbone!

ACTIVE **READING** As you read these two pages, find and underline the definition of *vertebrate*.

Animals that have a backbone are called **vertebrates**. There are many kinds of vertebrates. Frogs, birds, snakes, and tigers are all vertebrates. Vertebrates live in many places.

Lions live in grasslands. Their young are called cubs.

Fish

Fish are vertebrates, too. Fish are many sizes, shapes, and colors. Some fish are tiny. Other fish, such as the whale shark, are large. A whale shark can grow as long as a school bus! Fish take in oxygen through their gills and spend their whole lives in water.

Sea Horse

Male sea horses carry eggs in a part of their body called a pouch.

Monkfish

This fish lives deep in the ocean where there is no light.

Bass

This bass lives in fresh water. Like most kinds of fish, it lays eggs.

DO THE MATH

Measure in Centimeters

Alexa's goby is about 3 centimeters long. Draw a fish this long.

Samuel's goldfish is 6 centimeters long. Draw a fish this long.

Amphibian or Reptile?

How are amphibians and reptiles different? Read on to learn about these two groups.

ACTIVE **READING** As you read these two pages, draw circles around the clue words that signal when things are being compared.

Frog

This amphibian lives around water.

Turtle

This reptile lays eggs.

Amphibians [am•**FIB**•ee•uhnz] start life in water. Many amphibians move to land as they grow. Salamanders, toads, and frogs are amphibians. Like most other amphibians, frogs lay their eggs in water. When the eggs hatch, the tadpoles look like fish. Most amphibians have smooth, moist skin. Young amphibians have gills. Many adult amphibians have lungs.

Reptiles are animals with scales covering their bodies. Lizards and turtles are reptiles. Similar to amphibians, most reptiles hatch from eggs. A reptile breathes with lungs its whole life. Reptiles, such as crocodiles, that spend a lot of time in water must come up for air.

Identify

▶ Read the facts on each trading card. In the circles, write an "A" for amphibian or an "R" for reptile. Then color the borders green for reptiles or orange for amphibians.

Alligator

Alligators are covered with large scales. They lay eggs in nests.

Newt

Newts lay their eggs in water.

Gecko

Geckos are covered with scales. They breathe using lungs.

Frilled Lizard

R

Frilled lizards lay their eggs on the ground.

Mudpuppy

Mudpuppies have smooth, moist skin.

Salamander

A

Birds and Mammals

What are some other vertebrate groups? Read to find out.

ACTIVE **READING** As you read these two pages, underline three characteristics of birds and circle three characteristics of mammals.

Birds are another kind of vertebrate. Birds are animals that have wings, feathers, and beaks and lay eggs. Some birds, such as the hummingbird, are tiny. Other birds, such as the ostrich, are very large. Birds breathe with lungs.

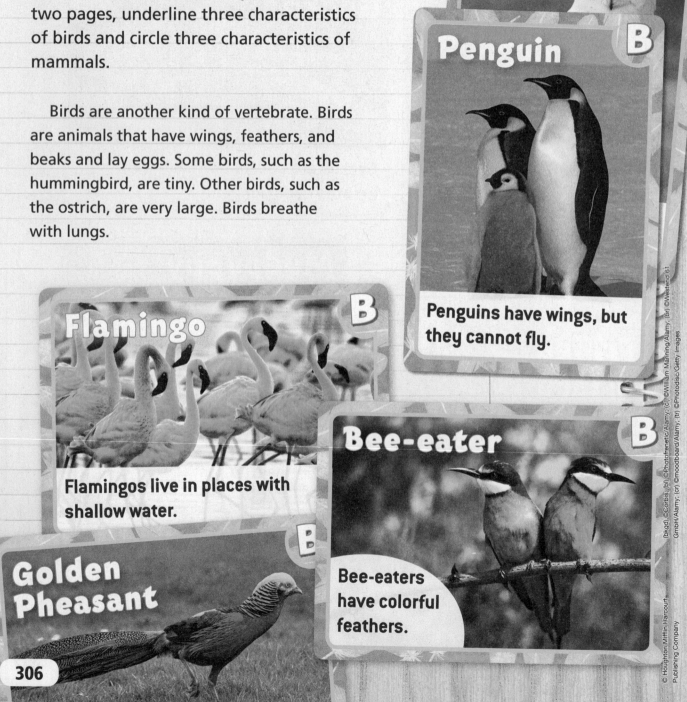

Owl B

Penguin B

Penguins have wings, but they cannot fly.

Flamingo B

Flamingos live in places with shallow water.

Bee-eater B

Bee-eaters have colorful feathers.

Golden Pheasant B

Elephants, apes, whales, and dolphins are all mammals. How are they alike? **Mammals** are animals that have fur or hair. Most do not lay eggs. Instead, female mammals give birth to live young and make milk to feed them. Mammals also use lungs to breathe.

Squirrel M

Bearded Seal M

Can you tell why this animal is called a bearded seal?

Kangaroo M

When a kangaroo is born, it crawls into its mother's pouch.

Emperor Tamarin M M

This monkey has hair covering its body.

▶ Draw your own bird or mammal card. Label its characteristics.

Black Bear M

Sum It Up »

Write the animal type on the line and then draw a line to the matching picture.

1   A _____ has fur or hair covering its body and gives birth to live young.

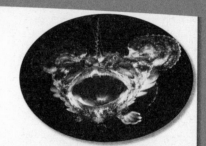

2   A _____ lives in water and takes in oxygen through gills.

3   A _____ lives on land or in water and has scales.

4   A _____ has feathers and wings.

5   An _____ has moist skin and begins life in the water.

Name _____

Vocabulary Review

1 Complete the maze to connect each animal to its classification at the bottom. Pass through each animal's traits along the way.

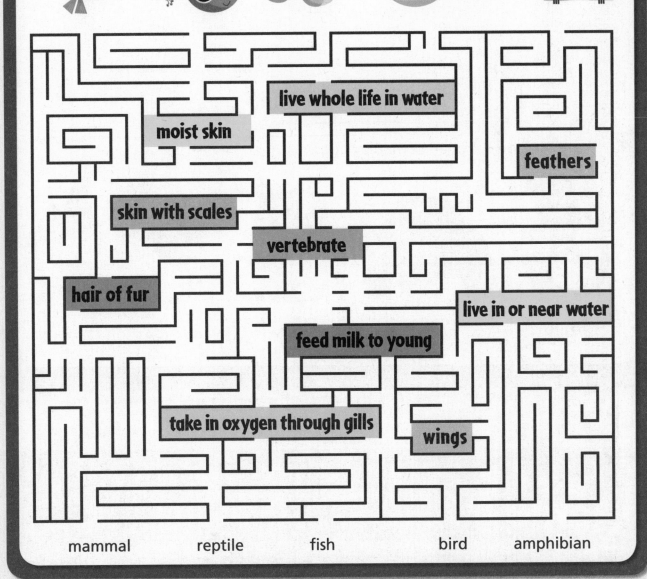

goldfish   salamander   snake   hippo   owl

live whole life in water

moist skin

feathers

skin with scales

vertebrate

hair of fur

live in or near water

feed milk to young

take in oxygen through gills

wings

mammal   reptile   fish   bird   amphibian

Apply Concepts

2 You are hiking along a river. You see an animal that looks like it could be either a lizard or a salamander. What are questions you could ask the guide to help you decide which animal it is?

_____

_____

_____

3 Draw an imaginary bird. Label the parts that make it a bird.

4 Place an X on the animals that lay eggs.

lizard   buffalo   newt   ostrich   salmon

Take It Home! Share what you learned about types of animals with a family member. Together, name and describe the fish, reptiles, amphibians, birds, and mammals you have seen or know about.

310

SC.3.L.15.1 Classify animals into major groups (mammals, birds, reptiles, amphibians, fish, arthropods, vertebrates and invertebrates, those having live births and those which lay eggs) according to their physical characteristics and behaviors. **SC.3.N.3.2** Recognize that scientists use models to help understand and explain how things work.

LESSON **3**

ESSENTIAL **QUESTION**

How Can We Classify Invertebrates?

 ## Engage Your Brain

Find the answer to the following question in this lesson and record it here.

Look at this "furry lobster." How do you know it is not a mammal?

_____

_____

_____

_____

_____

ACTIVE READING

Lesson Vocabulary

List each term. As you learn about each one, make notes in the Interactive Glossary.

_____

_____

_____

Main Idea and Details

Detail sentences give information about a topic. The information may be examples, features, characteristics, or facts. Active readers stay focused on the topic when they ask, What fact or information does this sentence add to the topic?

No Bones!

How are an octopus, lobster, cricket, and worm alike? They are all invertebrates.

ACTIVE **READING** As you read these two pages, find and underline lesson vocabulary each time it is used.

Invertebrates are animals without backbones. There are many kinds of invertebrates. Jellyfish, crabs, spiders, worms, and insects are some kinds. Invertebrates live in many places, from the ocean to your own backyard.

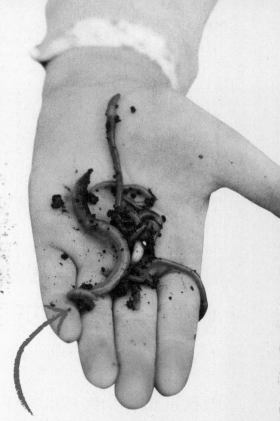

A worm has no backbone or hard outer covering.

The snail has a hard shell to protect its soft body.

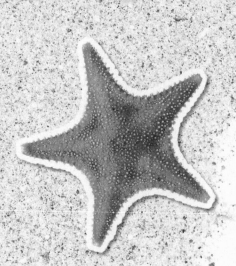

Most kinds of female sea stars release tiny eggs from each of their arms into ocean water.

This centipede has lots of legs!

► **Place an X beneath the pictures of invertebrates.**

Ladybugs lay tiny eggs on the undersides of leaves.

Arthropods

There are more types of arthropods than any other type of animal. What makes them special?

ACTIVE **READING** As you read these two pages, find and underline facts about insects.

Arthropods are invertebrates with jointed legs. Their bodies are divided into segments, or parts, and they have a hard, outer covering that protects them.

Insects are the largest group of arthropods. How can you tell which arthropods are insects? An insect's body has three main segments. Its head has two antennae. And it has six legs.

butterfly

walking stick

scorpion

▶ Find and circle these arthropods. Cross each off the list as you find it.

scorpion
butterfly
walking stick
spider
ant
tick
beetle

Spiders, scorpions, and crabs are arthropods, too. Yet they are not insects. Unlike insects, these arthropods only have two body parts. Insects always have six legs. But other kinds of arthropods have different numbers of legs.

beetle

tick

▶ Fill in the chart with the names of arthropods shown on these pages.

Arthropods

Insects

_____

_____

_____

Other Arthropods

_____

_____

_____

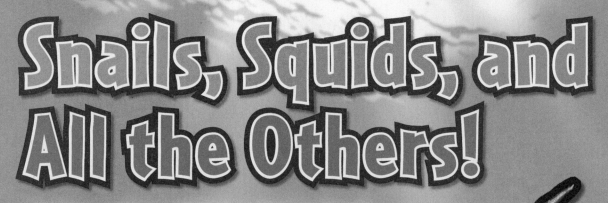

Snails, Squids, and All the Others!

Arthropods aren't the only kind of invertebrates. What other animals are invertebrates? Look and find out!

ACTIVE READING As you read these two pages, draw circles around the names of invertebrates.

Since a squid has no bones, it can fit its body in between rocks.

Periwinkles [PER•ih•wing•kuhlz] are saltwater snails.

Brittle stars live in the ocean and in pools near the shore.

DO THE **MATH**

Use Subtraction Facts

If 485 of every 500 animals are invertebrates, how many are vertebrates?

_____

_____

Like many invertebrates, sea slugs lay eggs.

When this octopus hatched from its egg, it was about the size of a housefly.

Anemones [uh•NEM•uh•neez] attach themselves to rocks or other surfaces.

A clam has a soft body with a hard shell to protect it.

Sum It Up »

The blue part of each summary statement is incorrect. Write words to replace the blue parts.

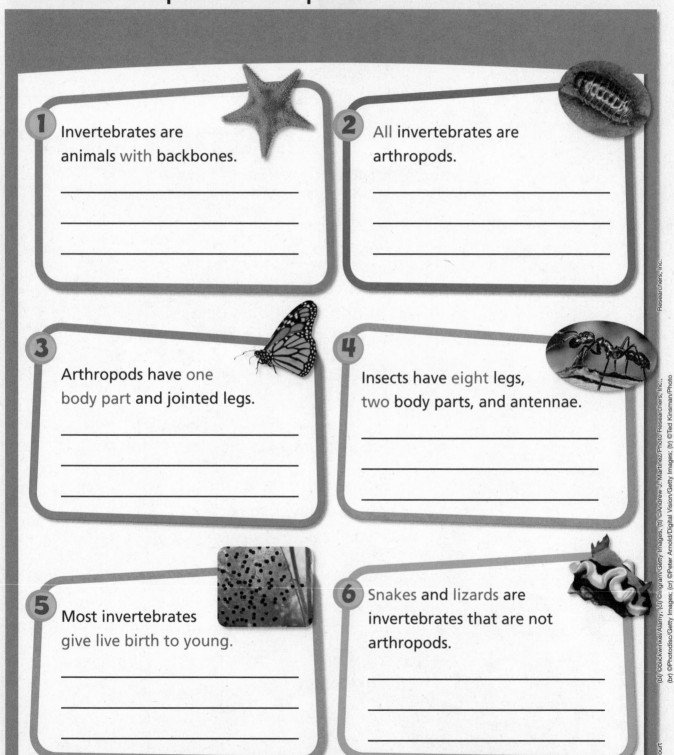

1 Invertebrates are animals with backbones.

_____
_____
_____

2 All invertebrates are arthropods.

_____
_____
_____

3 Arthropods have one body part and jointed legs.

_____
_____
_____

4 Insects have eight legs, two body parts, and antennae.

_____
_____
_____

5 Most invertebrates give live birth to young.

_____
_____
_____

6 Snakes and lizards are invertebrates that are not arthropods.

_____
_____
_____

Name _____

Vocabulary Review

1 Use the clues to fill in the missing letters of the words.

1. _ _ v _ _ _ _ _ _ _ _ _ _   the classification of an animal without a backbone

2. i _ _ _ _ _ t   an arthropod with six legs, three body parts, and antennae

3. _ _ _ t _ r _ _ _ _ _   an animal with jointed legs, a segmented body, and a hard outer covering

4. _ _ _ s   Most vertebrates lay ___.

5. _ o _ _ _ _ _ d   the kind of legs all arthropods have

6. c _ v _ _ _ _ _ g   All arthropods have a hard, outer _____.

7. _ _ _ t _ _ _ _ s   an ocean animal with eight legs that is not an arthropod

Apply Concepts

2 Look at the drawing of the scorpion. Complete the chart.

How many legs does it have?	
Does it have antennae?	
Does it have segmented body parts?	
Is it an arthropod?	
Is it an insect?	

3 Draw an arthropod of your choice. Write what makes it an arthropod.

_____

_____

_____

_____

_____

Take It Home! Make a poster to show different invertebrates. Group them as *arthropods or not arthropods*. Use labels to show the differences between the two groups.

PEOPLE **IN SCIENCE**

Meet the
Insect Scientists

Oscar Liburd

Liburd studies pests that attack small fruit plants.

Oscar Liburd is an entomologist. He studies insects and other pests that harm small fruit plants. He finds ways to control pests without harmful chemicals. Liburd also uses pesticides that are safer for people. In 1999, Liburd started teaching about pest control. His work today helps Florida's farmers keep pests away from their crops.

Charles Henry Turner

Charles Turner was an entomologist. He studied many kinds of insects, including ants and wasps. Turner studied honeybees, too. In 1910, he proved that honeybees can see color. The next year he proved they could also see patterns. Turner found that some ants move in circles toward their home. To honor his work with ants, scientists call this behavior "Turner's circling."

Turner showed that honeybees can see a flower's color.

The Insect Scientist

Read the timeline below. Use what you read about Liburd and Turner to fill in each blank box.

1997 Liburd graduates from the University of Rhode Island.

1910 Turner proves that honeybees can see color.

1907 Charles Turner writes about his study of ants.

Think About It!

After what year on the timeline should you add the following?

A scientist names the circles ants make when returning home "Turner's circling."

SC.3.L.15.1 Classify animals into major groups... SC.3.L.15.2 Classify flowering and non-flowering plants into major groups... SC.3.N.1.1 Raise questions about the natural world, investigate them... SC.3.N.1.7 Explain that empirical evidence is...used to help validate explanations of natural phenomena.

(i) INQUIRY LESSON 4

Name _____

ESSENTIAL QUESTION

How Do You Classify Things?

EXPLORE

In this activity, you will classify plants and animals.

Before You Begin—Preview the Steps

1 Decide how you will group the plants or animals.

2 From the magazines, cut out pictures that belong in your groups. CAUTION: Be careful with the scissors.

3 Sort the pictures into the groups you chose.

4 Glue the sorted pictures onto poster board. Label each plant or animal group. Be prepared to explain your groupings.

Materials

magazines
scissors
glue
poster board
markers, crayons, or colored pencils

323

Set a Purpose

What are some ways that you can group plants or animals?

_____

_____

_____

Think About the Procedure

How will you show the different groupings on your poster?

_____

_____

What characteristics will you use to classify the plants or animals?

_____

_____

_____

_____

Name _____

Record Your Data

Design your poster and describe your categories in the space below.

Draw Conclusions

Why is classifying plants and animals by their characteristics helpful?

_____

_____

_____

Claims • Evidence • Reasoning

1. Compare your groupings with those of other student groups. How were they the same? How were they different?

_____

_____

_____

2. If scientists discovered a new plant, what evidence would help them support a claim that the plant was a non-flowering plant?

_____

_____

3. If scientists discovered a new animal in a rain forest, what kinds of evidence would help classify the animal?

_____

_____

_____

_____

4. What might make it difficult to classify some types of plants or animals using photos? Explain your reasoning.

_____

_____

_____

_____

5. Think of other questions you might like to ask about classifying plants or animals.

_____

_____

_____

Name _____

Vocabulary Review

Use the terms in the box to complete the sentences.

| mammal |
| insect |
| invertebrate |
| vertebrate |

1. A(n) _____ has a backbone.

2. A(n) _____ does not have a backbone.

3. A(n) _____ is an arthropod because it has jointed legs.

4. You can tell a fox is a(n) _____ because it has fur.

Science Concepts

Fill in the letter of the choice that best answers the question.

5. On a visit to a beach, Hasna sees many sea animals. Which of the sea animals is a vertebrate?

   (A) clam   (C) sea snail

   (B) crab   (D) sea turtle

6. Look at the illustration of a jellyfish.

   Which of the following features is used as evidence to classify this animal as an invertebrate?

   (F) tentacles

   (G) soft body parts

   (H) has a skeleton

   (I) does not have a backbone

7. There are many different types of invertebrates. Which two invertebrates would belong in the same group?

   (A) jellyfish and spider

   (B) ant and snail

   (C) octopus and tick

   (D) beetle and walking stick

8. The table below lists some of the Florida state animals.

Title	Animal
State horse	cracker horse
State fish	largemouth bass
State bird	mockingbird
State insect	zebra longwing butterfly

   Which of the following animals is an arthropod?

   (F) cracker horse   (H) mockingbird

   (G) largemouth bass   (I) zebra longwing butterfly

9. Juan wants to study arthropods by making a model. Which type of animal should he model?

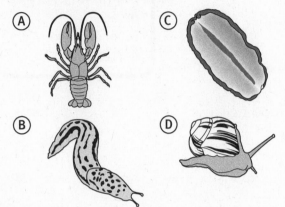

Ⓐ Ⓒ

Ⓑ Ⓓ

10. The carpenter ant is one of the more common insects found in Florida homes. The diagram below shows the life cycle of the carpenter ant.

Life Cycle of the Carpenter Ant

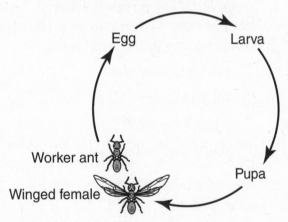

Egg → Larva

Worker ant

Winged female

Pupa

Octavio observes the diagram and says the carpenter ant is an arthropod. What could he use as evidence?

Ⓕ It hatches from an egg.

Ⓖ The female has wings and can fly.

Ⓗ The male and female look different.

Ⓘ It has a body divided into smaller parts.

11. Zach uses a hand lens to examine the petals of a plant. What can Zach conclude about the plant that produced the petals?

Ⓐ It is a fern plant.

Ⓑ It is a moss plant.

Ⓒ It is a flowering plant.

Ⓓ It is a nonflowering plant.

12. Sungwan makes a booklet about different animals. The picture shows the animals she describes in her booklet.

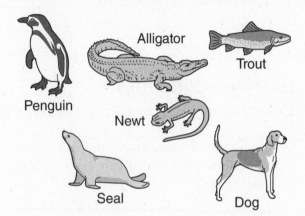

Penguin · Alligator · Trout · Newt · Seal · Dog

Which two of these animals are the same type of vertebrate?

Ⓕ dog and seal

Ⓖ seal and trout

Ⓗ trout and penguin

Ⓘ alligator and newt

328 **Unit 8**

Name _____

13. Dylan has a pet toad like the one in the picture. He reads a book to learn more about it. He finds out that adult toads use lungs to breathe.

Which of these animals breathes in a way that is different from the way an adult toad breathes?

(A) bear

(B) crocodile

(C) duck

(D) parrotfish

14. Nori is making a model of an insect. What will she need to include in the model to make it correct?

(F) wings

(G) six legs

(H) backbone

(I) eight legs

15. Jamal hikes in the woods. He finds a pine cone on the hiking trail. What can Jamal conclude about the type of plant that produced the cone?

(A) It is a fern plant.

(B) It is a moss plant.

(C) It is a flowering plant.

(D) It is a nonflowering plant.

16. Marty knows that two plants listed in the table below produce spores.

1	cone-bearing plants
2	fern plants
3	flowering plants
4	moss plants

Which of the following two plants produce spores?

(F) 1 and 2

(G) 1 and 3

(H) 2 and 3

(I) 2 and 4

17. Sanjoy reads a book about desert animals. He thinks the most interesting animal is a mountain lion. Which other animal described in the book is the same type of vertebrate as a mountain lion?

(A) spiny lizard

(B) kangaroo rat

(C) long-eared owl

(D) monarch butterfly

18. Emi sorts plants into groups. The table below shows how she groups the plants.

Group 1	Group 2
sequoia	moss
maple tree	boston fern
lily	

What would be a correct title for Group 1?

(F) flowering plants

(G) nonflowering plants

(H) seed-producing plants

(I) spore-producing plants

Apply Inquiry and Review the Big Idea

Write the answers to these questions.

19. Ulrich wants to classify the plants shown below based on their leaves.

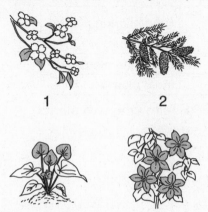

1

2

3

4

Make a claim about which plant does not belong in this group. Cite evidence to support your claim, and explain your reasoning.

_____

_____

_____

20. Silvio has a conifer and an apple tree in his front yard. Silvio says that the two plants are classified in two different plant groups. What is the main difference between the groups the conifer and apple tree belong to?

_____

_____

_____

21. Coreen has a tree house in her backyard. When she plays there, she sees many small animals. She sees squirrels, bluebirds, flies, inchworms, and spiders. Which of the animals that she has seen are vertebrates, and which are invertebrates? Give reasons for your classifications.

_____

_____

_____

Living Things Change

FLORIDA BIG IDEA 17

Interdependence

Animals find food in the ocean.

I Wonder Why

This turtle catches jellyfish to eat. Other animals also eat plants or animals. Why? *Turn the page to find out.*

Here's Why

Living things need energy to live, grow, and change. Animals get energy from eating plants or other animals—or both.

Essential Questions and Florida Benchmarks

 Science Notebook

Before you begin each lesson, write your thoughts about the Essential Question.

SC.3.L.17.1 Describe how animals and plants respond to changing seasons.

LESSON 1

ESSENTIAL **QUESTION**

How Do Living Things Change with the Seasons?

 Engage Your Brain

Find the answer to the following question in this lesson and record it here.

This young loggerhead turtle has just hatched. During which season did this most likely happen?

_____

_____

📖 ACTIVE **READING**

Lesson Vocabulary

List terms. As you learn about each one, make notes in the Interactive Glossary.

_____

_____

_____

Visual Aids

A picture adds information to the text that appears on the page with it. Active readers pause their reading to review the picture and decide how the information in it adds to what is provided in the text.

Spring Has Sprung!

Many places on Earth have four seasons. In those places, animals and plants change throughout the seasons of spring, summer, fall, and winter.

ACTIVE **READING** As you read these pages, draw two lines under the main idea in each paragraph.

Spring is a time for growth and change. You might see tiny plants growing out of the soil. The sprouting of a seed is called **germination** [jer•muh•NAY•shuhn]. The buds on trees and shrubs open into leaves and flowers.

Animals also respond to the seasonal changes of spring. Many animals reproduce, or have their young, in spring. Perhaps you have seen young birds in a nest in the spring. In spring, some kinds of animals **migrate**, or move from one place to another. They move to find food or to reproduce.

Get growing! Many plants, such as this crocus, sprout and grow in springtime.

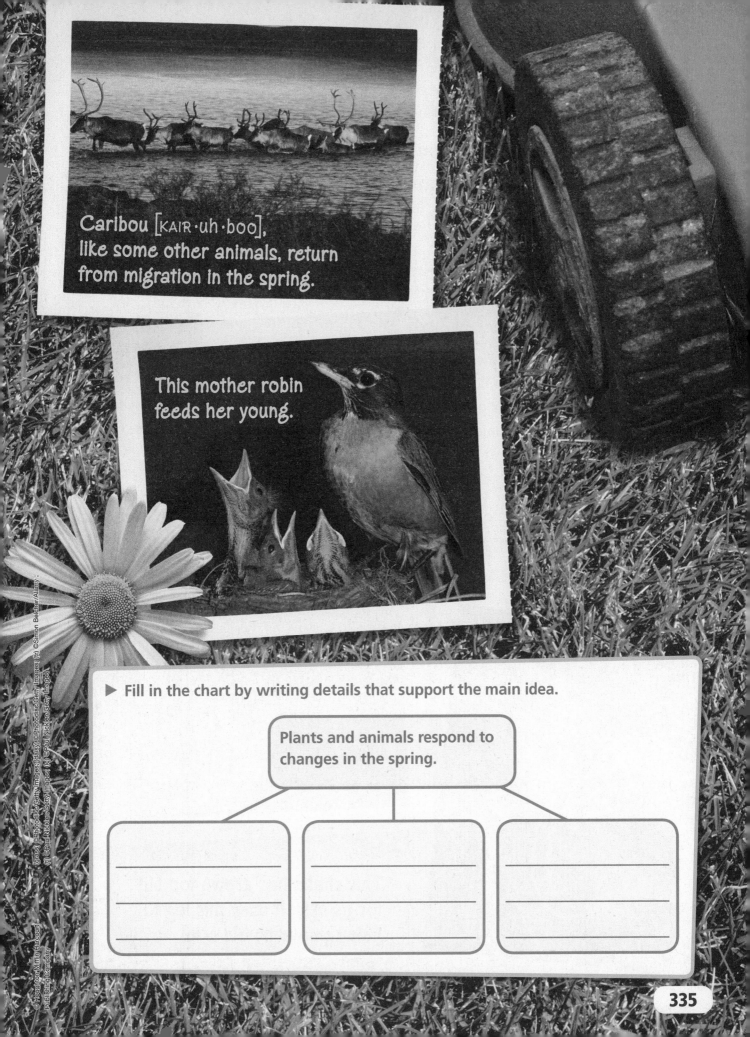

Caribou [KAIR·uh·boo], like some other animals, return from migration in the spring.

This mother robin feeds her young.

► Fill in the chart by writing details that support the main idea.

Plants and animals respond to changes in the spring.

Summertime!

With summer comes warmer weather and lots of daylight. Plants and animals grow and change in summertime.

ACTIVE **READING** As you read these pages, draw a line under two details about what some living things do in summer.

In summer, many kinds of plants grow flowers. Fruits grow from parts of the flowers. The fruits contain seeds. In summer, young animals grow and become stronger. By late summer, some young animals leave the care of their parents.

These young robins grow and become stronger in the summer.

This snake has grown too big for its skin. It uses this log to help remove its old skin.

A cherry tree flowers in the spring. In summer, the flowers grow into red, ripe cherries!

This loggerhead turtle comes out of the sea to lay her eggs. The eggs hatch in about 60 days.

Many insects grow and change in the summer.

▶ What would your garden look like in summertime? Draw a picture of your garden.

Harvest Time

In fall, many plants and animals respond to cooler weather and fewer hours of daylight.

ACTIVE **READING** As you read these pages, draw one line under a cause. Draw two lines under an effect.

Some trees respond to the changes of fall by dropping nuts or fruits. The leaves may also turn color and fall to the ground. Many vegetables are ready for harvest now.

Some animals respond to fall's seasonal changes, too. Some gather and store food. The fur on some animals may get thicker and change color. Other animals migrate.

Ripe fruits and vegetables are harvested, or picked, and sent to market.

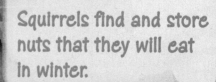

Squirrels find and store nuts that they will eat in winter.

Geese migrate to warmer places in the fall.

The leaves of some trees change color in fall. One by one, the leaves fall off. Then the tree is bare.

Young loggerhead turtles hatch and head for the sea.

DO THE **MATH**

Solve a Two-Step Problem

A squirrel stores 300 nuts in a nest. It buries another 500 nuts. In winter, it eats 350 nuts. How many nuts are left?

_____

_____

Winter Days!

In many places, snow and ice cover the ground in winter. Plants and animals respond to the cold winter weather in different ways.

ACTIVE **READING** As you read these two pages, draw a line under the words that describe what the photos are showing.

In many places, food is scarce in winter. To survive, some kinds of animals **hibernate**. This means they move little and use little energy during the winter. They live off stored body fat. The heart rate slows and body temperature drops.

Dormice (top photo) and hedgehogs hibernate in nests. The frog is hibernating under the water of a pond. Even some insects, like these ladybugs, hibernate!

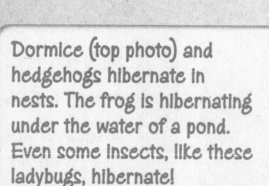

This tree has lost its leaves. It is dormant in winter.

By wintertime, most trees and bushes have lost their leaves. Without leaves, plants cannot make food for themselves. Growth slows or may even stop. These trees and bushes are said to be *dormant*. They will grow again in the spring.

▶ Compare what animals do in winter with what they do in another season.

Winter	_____

Sum It Up »

Complete the graphic organizer with details from the summary below.

Plants and animals change with the seasons. During spring, many seeds germinate, buds open, and many animals have their young. Summer is a time when plants and young animals grow and become strong. In fall, leaves fall from trees, crops are harvested, and animals prepare for winter. Some animals hibernate during winter, and some plants are dormant.

1 Spring

_____
_____
_____

2 Summer

_____
_____
_____

Main Idea: Plants and animals change with the seasons.

3 Fall

_____
_____
_____

4 Winter

_____
_____
_____

Vocabulary Review

1 Fill in the missing letters to find each word. You will use each of the letters below.

E E E G G I I
L M N N R T T T

1. H __ B E __ __ A __ E
2. V E __ E __ A B __ __ S
3. M __ __ R A __ __
4. G __ R __ I __ A T __ O N

Fill in the blanks with the correct word from above.

5. In winter, some animals _____ and use very little energy.

6. In springtime, _____ of many kinds of seeds takes place.

7. Animals travel from one place to another, or _____, to find food or to reproduce.

8. Many kinds of ripe fruits and _____ are harvested in the fall.

2 Look at the pictures. Write the season shown and how the plant or animal responds.

_____   _____   _____

_____   _____   _____

3 Choose one season that you read about. Draw a picture of how a plant responds to changes in that season. Draw a picture of how an animal might respond. Then describe your pictures.

Plant Response

Animal Response

_____   _____

_____   _____

_____   _____

Take It Home!

See *ScienceSaurus®* for more information about living things and seasons.

SC.3.L.17.2 Recognize that plants use energy from the Sun, air, and water to make their own food. **SC.3.N.1.1** Raise questions about the natural world, investigate them . . . **SC.3.N.1.3** Keep records as appropriate . . . **SC.3.N.1.6** Infer based on observation.

INQUIRY
LESSON 2

Name _____

ESSENTIAL QUESTION

What Do Plants Need?

EXPLORE

Grrr! When your stomach growls, you know you're hungry. You might grab an apple to eat. Food is one of the things you need to live. What is one thing plants need to live?

Before You Begin—Preview the Steps

1 Label one plant **A**. Put this plant in a place that gets a lot of light.

2 Label the second plant **B**. Put this plant in a dark place.

3 Use the measuring cup to give each plant the same amount of water. Keep the plants where they are for two weeks. Record your observations.

Set a Purpose

What do you think you will learn from this experiment?

_____

_____

_____

State Your Hypothesis

Write your hypothesis, or testable statement, about what will happen to each plant.

_____

_____

_____

_____

Think About the Procedure

Why is it important to place one plant in light and one plant in darkness and keep everything else the same?

_____

_____

_____

Which variable are you testing?

_____

What kinds of things will you observe about the plants?

_____

_____

_____

Name _____

Record Your Data

In the space below, make a data table and record your observations.

[blank box]

Draw Conclusions

What did you observe about plant *A*? What did you observe about plant *B*?

_____

_____

_____

Why did you need to observe the plants for a full two weeks?

_____

_____

_____

Claims • Evidence • Reasoning

1. Write a claim based on your hypothesis. Cite evidence that supports
   your claim and explain your reasoning.

   _____

   _____

   _____

   _____

   _____

2. Write a claim about how light affects plants. Cite evidence that
   supports your claim and explain your reasoning.

   _____

   _____

   _____

   _____

3. You gave both plants the same amount of water. Explain your
   reasoning.

   _____

   _____

   _____

4. Think of other questions to ask about the needs of plants.

   _____

   _____

SC.3.L.17.1 Describe how animals and plants respond to changing seasons. **SC.3.N.1.1** Raise questions about the natural world, investigate them individually and in teams through free exploration and systematic investigations, and generate appropriate explanations based on those explorations.

Meet the Nature Scientists

Margaret Morse Nice

Margaret Morse Nice studied birds. For years, Nice watched the song sparrows in her yard. She kept notes on how birds mated, built nests, and raised their young. She studied how they migrate as the seasons change. Nice wrote scientific articles about her studies of birds.

Nice tagged birds with a colored band to track each bird through its life.

Luther Burbank

Luther Burbank wanted to improve the world's food supply. He experimented with fruits, vegetables, and flowers. To make a new kind of plant, Burbank combined two different plants. One famous plant that Burbank made was the Burbank potato. This potato was larger than other potatoes. Today it is known as the Idaho potato.

Burbank combined a plum and an apricot to make a plumcot.

Be a Birdwatcher!

Label each bird with the number of the matching clue.

1 You see a small, brown-and-white bird. It is singing a pretty song.

2 You hear a tapping sound in a tree. It is a red-headed bird finding insects in the wood.

3 A bright red bird with a black face sits on a branch. Its beak is red and shaped like a cone.

4 You hear a noisy bird. The noise is made by a large bird with blue, white, and black feathers.

5 A flash of green and red flies by. It is a small bird with a long, thin beak.

6 An orange bird with a black head is up high in a tree.

7 A glossy-black bird sits on a branch. It has a red and yellow mark on each shoulder.

SC.3.L.17.2 Recognize that plants use energy from the Sun, air, and water to make their own food.

LESSON 3

ESSENTIAL **QUESTION**

How Do Plants and Animals Get Energy?

 Engage Your Brain

Find the answer to the following question in this lesson and record it here.

What do these two animals and the grasses have in common?

_____

_____

📖 ACTIVE **READING**

Lesson Vocabulary

List terms. As you learn about each one, make notes in the Interactive Glossary.

_____

_____

_____

_____

Sequence

Many ideas in this lesson are connected by a sequence, or order, that describes the steps in a process. Active readers stay focused on sequence when they mark the transition from one step in a process to another.

351

Soak Up the Sun

Plants need energy to grow and reproduce. Where do you think this energy comes from?

ACTIVE **READING** As you read these pages, draw one line under the source of energy for producers. Draw two lines under the products of photosynthesis that contain energy.

sunlight

You eat food, such as tomatoes, to get energy. But all green plants, like these tomato plants, must produce, or make, their own food. A **producer** is a living thing that makes its own food.

The process a plant uses to make food is called **photosynthesis** [foht•oh•**SIN**•thuh•sis]. During photosynthesis, plants use the energy from sunlight to change water and carbon dioxide [dy•**AHKS**•yd], a gas in the air, into sugars. A plant uses the sugars as food for growth, or it stores them. During photosynthesis, plants give off oxygen, a gas animals need to breathe.

Photosynthesis happens in leaves. The sun's energy is used to make sugars, which the plant uses or stores.

▶ **What does a plant take in for photosynthesis? What does the plant produce?**

Plants Take In	Plants Produce

water

carbon dioxide

When we eat tomatoes, we get energy from the sugars a tomato plant made and stored!

Mesquite trees use energy from the sun to produce sugars. They store some of the sugars in their seeds.

Nature's Dinnertime

Plants use the sun's energy to make food. Where do you think animals get the energy they need to survive?

ACTIVE **READING** As you read these two pages, write numbers next to the appropriate pictures to show the order of events in the food chain.

Animals get their energy by eating plants or by eating other animals. A **consumer** is a living thing that eats other living things. All animals are consumers. Some animals, such as rabbits and deer, eat only plants. They are *herbivores* [**HUR**•buh•vohrz]. Some animals, such as wolves and dolphins, eat only other animals. They are *carnivores* [**KAR**•nuh•vohrz]. The energy stored in food is passed from plants to animals in a **food chain**. Animals use the energy from food to live and grow.

Food chains are found everywhere on Earth. They are in the ocean, rain forests, grasslands, and deserts. Food chains first begin with producers. Consumers come next in a food chain.

Kangaroo rats get energy by consuming mesquite seeds.

Rattlesnakes eat kangaroo rats to get energy.

The roadrunner is the consumer at the top of this food chain. The energy stored in food passes through the food chain to the roadrunner.

▶ Draw the missing part in the food chain. Then label the producer and the consumers.

What's for Dinner?

You may have had corn on the cob at a picnic. Corn and other plants grown as food are known as crops.

Crops such as corn, wheat, and barley are grains grown on farms all over the United States. Crops are food for people. Crops are also food for livestock, such as cows, pigs, and chickens. Livestock are also raised as food for people. Farmers grow grains to feed livestock. The crops grown by farmers are an important part of a food chain.

Corn is a producer.

Chickens are consumers. They eat corn.

Farmers must meet the needs of plants in order for crops to grow. Crops must get plenty of air, sunlight, and water. To get water to the crops, farmers may dig long ditches. Water is pumped through the ditches to the crops. Farmers also might use sprinklers to water crops.

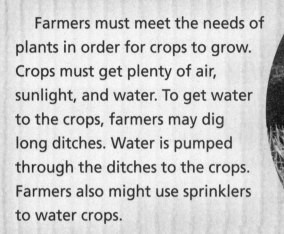

Sprinkler irrigation brings water to this crop of corn.

DO THE MATH
Solve a Word Problem

It takes 8 pounds of corn to feed 40 chickens each day. How many pounds of corn does it take to feed 40 chickens in one week?

_____

_____

_____

You are a consumer who might eat corn, chicken, or both.

Sum It Up »

Find and circle the incorrect word in each summary statement. Write the correct word on the line.

1 Plants need carbon dioxide from the air, water, and oxygen to make food.

_____

2 Plants store food in the form of water.

_____
_____

3 A living thing that eats plants or animals is a producer.

_____
_____

4 A food chain shows the path of energy from consumers to animals.

_____

5 Crops are at the beginning of an important food grain.

_____
_____

Name _____

Vocabulary Review

1 Use the clues to unscramble the words in the box. Use the word bank if you need help.

1. reracvoin: an animal that eats only other animal	
2. rprecduo: a living thing that makes its own food	
3. ofod incah: the path of energy through living things	
4. srsuag: what plants make during photosyntheis	
5. monusrce: a living thing that eats other living things	
6. ssthphooeinyts: the process plants use to make food	
7. bihrereov: an animal that eats only plants	

2 Look at the picture of the food chain below. Label each producer and consumer.

_____ _____ _____

3 Look at the picture of a plant. Draw an X where the plant makes food.

4 What two things does a plant make during photosynthesis?

_____

List what a plant needs for photosynthesis.

_____

_____

5 Think about some foods you eat. Draw a food chain in which you are the last link.

_____

_____

 What crops do you eat? Make a list. Ask members of your family to add to your list. Find out where these crops come from. Are they local, or are they from far away?

SC.3.N.3.2 Recognize that scientists use models to help understand and explain how things work. SC.3.N.3.3 Recognize that all models are approximations of natural phenomena; as such, they do not perfectly account for all observations.

S.T.E.M.

ENGINEERING & TECHNOLOGY

Save It for Later:
Food Preservation

Long ago, people learned to save, or preserve, food. First, people used nature to help them preserve food. Then, people made tools and processes to help. Follow the timeline to see how food preservation has changed over time.

5,000 Years Ago

Salt preserved meat. Ice kept food from spoiling. People dried meat and fruit.

1855

In an icebox, air flowed around a block of ice like this one. The cool air kept food fresh.

1795

Heating foods in glass jars kept them fresh. Preserving foods in glass jars and metal cans became common.

What types of food preservation are still used today? Why are older ways still used even though we have newer tools?

_____

_____

_____

Analyze a Product

Grocery stores are filled with products that are preserved for freshness. Think about a favorite product you buy in the grocery store.

Frozen dinners last about six months.

1900s

Refrigerators became common in the 1940s. Before the 1990s, most refrigerators used gases that harmed the atmosphere.

How is your favorite product preserved? How does the package help it stay fresh? How long does it last after you open it?

_____

_____

_____

_____

_____

ENGINEERING DESIGN CHALLENGE

Solve It:
Helping Animals Migrate

Every fall, caribou migrate. They travel from their summer home to their winter home. In the spring, they migrate in the opposite direction. A highway will soon be built across the middle of the migration route. People are afraid that the caribou will not be able to safely cross the highway.

Caution:
Caribou
crossing

DESIGN PROCESS STEPS

1 Find a Problem
2 Plan & Build
3 Test & Improve
4 Redesign
5 Communicate

What to Do:

1. Learn about caribou migration.

2. Build a model that shows the winter and summer home of a caribou herd.

3. Make a road that blocks the migration route.

4. Think of ways that the caribou can travel safely across the road. List three ideas.

5. Choose one of the ideas.

6. Build a model of your migration helper. Describe your solution and explain how it helps the caribou.

7. Draw your solution in your Science Notebook.

Name _____

Vocabulary Review

Check the box to show whether each statement is about a consumer or a producer or both.

Producer	Consumer	
☐	☐	1. the type of organism that grass is
☐	☐	2. the type of organism that eats plants
☐	☐	3. the type of organism that needs energy to live

Science Concepts

Fill in the letter of the choice that best answers the question.

4. Kadim planted bean seeds in four jars with soil. He kept the jars in different places in his bedroom. For 3 weeks, he put the same amount of water into each jar. He drew these pictures to show the rest of his class how the plants looked.

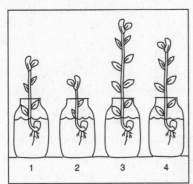

Based on the pictures, which plant was in the darkest place in Kadim's bedroom?

(A) Plant 1   (C) Plant 4

(B) Plant 2   (D) Plant 3

5. Julie put a plant under a growth light, watered the plant, and it grew well. Then there was a power failure at school for one week. When school reopened, Julie's plant was the same size, but many leaves were yellow. Which sentence best tells what happened to the plant?

(F) The plant grew well during the power failure.

(G) The plant got no light during the power failure.

(H) The plant did not change during the power failure.

(I) The plant got too much light during the power failure.

6. Kobe must write a report about how some plants or animals respond to seasonal changes during the fall. Which topic should Kobe choose for his report?

Ⓐ migration

Ⓑ germination

Ⓒ hibernation

Ⓓ dormancy

7. A food chain shows how living things depend on other living things for energy. Which of the following correctly shows how energy moves through a food chain?

Ⓕ grass ⟶ oak tree ⟶ human

Ⓖ grass ⟶ chicken ⟶ human

Ⓗ human ⟶ chicken ⟶ grass

Ⓘ chicken ⟶ grass ⟶ human

8. Plants get energy from the sun. Plants without sunlight will not grow. How do plants use energy from the sun?

Ⓐ to make their own food

Ⓑ to get rid of nutrients

Ⓒ to change water into sunlight

Ⓓ to change water into minerals

9. During the fall, many geese migrate to places with warm temperatures. Why do geese migrate?

Ⓕ They look for snowy weather.

Ⓖ They look for food sources.

Ⓗ They look for dormant trees.

Ⓘ They look for places to hibernate.

10. During the cold winter season, Ellen knows that changes happen in nature. Which of the following happens where winter is very cold?

Ⓐ Plants form flowers.

Ⓑ Most plants germinate.

Ⓒ Some animals hibernate.

Ⓓ Most animals reproduce.

11. The picture below shows a food chain in the ocean.

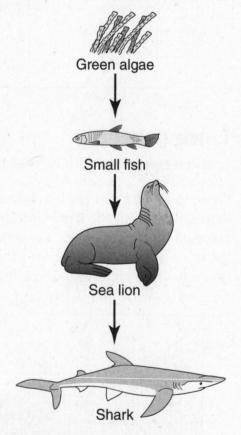

Green algae

Small fish

Sea lion

Shark

How does the small fish get energy?

Ⓕ by eating algae

Ⓖ by eating the shark

Ⓗ by photosynthesis

Ⓘ by eating the sea lion

Name _____

12. Mindy makes a poster about plants and animals during the spring. She wants to show how they respond to changes in the environment. Which picture does Mindy include on her poster?

Ⓐ   Ⓒ

Ⓑ   Ⓓ

13. During the winter, a frog burrows in the mud to hibernate. What happens to the frog while it hibernates?

Ⓕ It uses less energy.

Ⓖ It uses more energy.

Ⓗ Its heartbeat speeds up.

Ⓘ Its body fat increases.

14. Study these tree branches in the pictures below. Which tree branch would you see during the summer season?

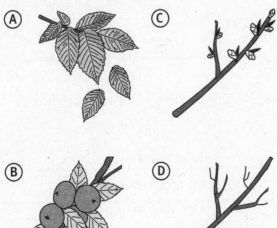

Ⓐ   Ⓒ

Ⓑ   Ⓓ

15. Shanaz knows that many types of birds migrate in response to seasonal changes. During which two seasons will Shanaz see birds migrating?

Ⓕ fall and winter

Ⓖ spring and summer

Ⓗ summer and fall

Ⓘ spring and fall

16. In the table below, Charlotte lists some ways that animals respond to seasonal changes in the environment.

1	migrate
2	hibernate
3	reproduce
4	gather food

Which happen during the fall season?

Ⓐ 1 and 2 only   Ⓒ 2 and 3 only

Ⓑ 1 and 3 only   Ⓓ 1 and 4 only

17. Study the pictures below of animals in different environments. Which activity happens during the cold winter season?

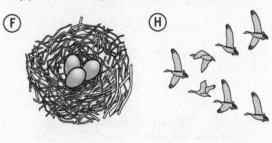
Ⓕ   Ⓗ

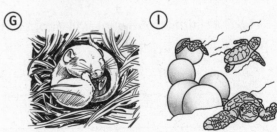
Ⓖ   Ⓘ

Apply Inquiry and Review the Big Idea

Write the answers to these questions.

18. In the table below, Adam lists reasons why birds migrate during the fall.

1	to find food
2	to gather and store food
3	to find warm weather
4	to find a place to hibernate

Make a claim about which two reasons are correct. Cite evidence to support your claim.

_____

_____

_____

19. A food chain, like the one below, shows how energy moves between things.

? ⟶ rabbit ⟶ fox

Identify a living thing that could replace the question mark. Explain your reasoning.

_____

_____

20. Study the winter scene shown below.

Make a claim about what will happen to the tree as it goes through spring, summer, and fall.

_____

_____

Computer technology is all around us. You can use a desktop computer to study math, listen to music, or keep in touch with family. Many other devices, such as cell phones and digital cameras and camcorders, contain computer technology, too. How does this technology work? What problems can it solve? If you are interested in these questions, you might like computer science. *Computer science* is the study of computer technology.

ACTIVE **READING**

As you read, underline examples of tools and devices that use computer technology.

Computers at work...

The word *compute* means to *do math.* Computers are devices that do math and perform tasks. For this reason, they are useful for many purposes. Biologists can use computers to record and analyze data about wildlife. Artists can use computers to model lifelike animations. Computer scientists study and develop computer technology. They might use their knowledge to improve existing devices or to create new ones.

What are some ways that you use computers?

_____

_____

_____

_____

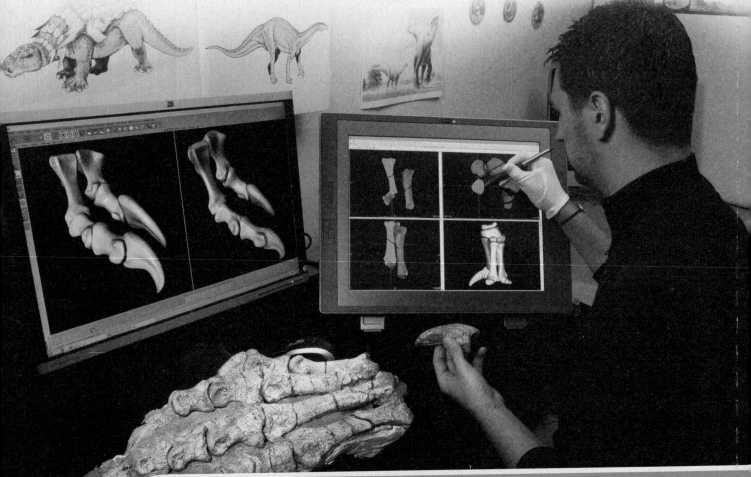

Many fields, such as medicine and education, rely on some kind of computer technology. Computer scientists can apply their skills to many different tasks. Working in computer science is a bit like solving a puzzle. Computer scientists think logically and creatively to solve problems. They often collaborate with others.

The students pictured here are using computer technology to build something fun: a robotic vehicle!

Let's talk

Computers carry out tasks by following instructions, or programs, that people design. Examples of computer programs include websites, mobile games, and digital photo editors. Computer programs are sometimes called *software*, *applications*, or *apps*.

Computer programs are not written in human language. They are written in a special programming language, or *code*, that the computer can interpret. If you learn how to write code, you can write computer programs, too!

```
15
16   # Check if player has grown 5 tomatoes and 5 carrots
17   if tomato_count >= 5 and carrot_count >= 5:
18       print ("Congratulations! Get ready for Round 2.")
19   else:
         print ("Keep working on your garden.")
```

If you want to work with computers, you need to learn to speak their language

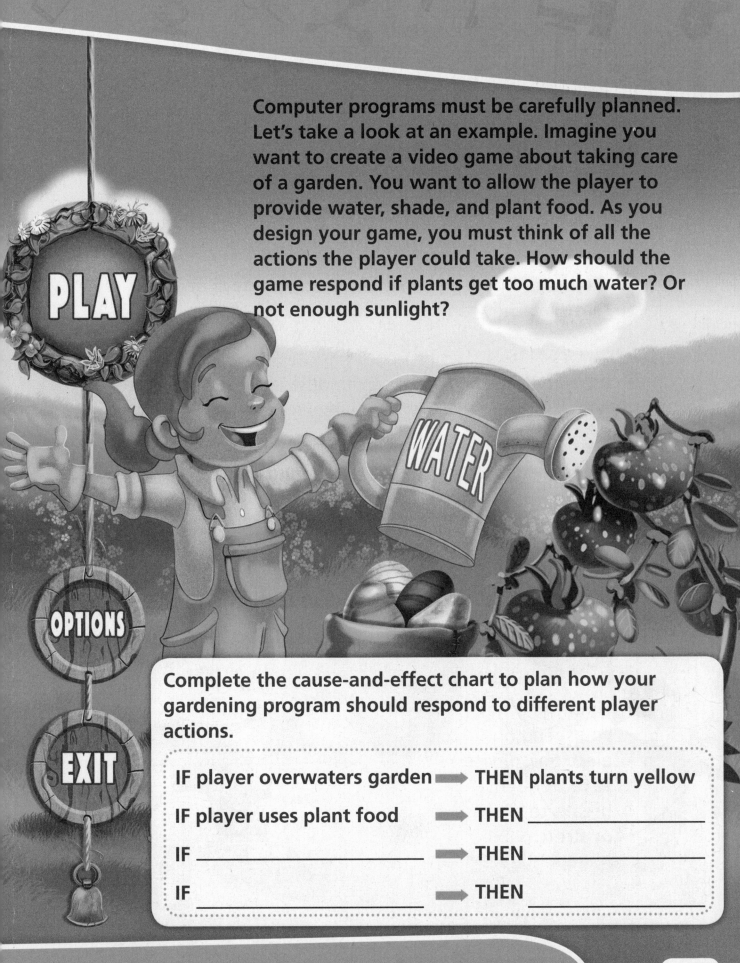

Computer programs must be carefully planned. Let's take a look at an example. Imagine you want to create a video game about taking care of a garden. You want to allow the player to provide water, shade, and plant food. As you design your game, you must think of all the actions the player could take. How should the game respond if plants get too much water? Or not enough sunlight?

PLAY

OPTIONS

EXIT

Complete the cause-and-effect chart to plan how your gardening program should respond to different player actions.

IF player overwaters garden ⟹ THEN plants turn yellow

IF player uses plant food ⟹ THEN _____

IF _____ ⟹ THEN _____

IF _____ ⟹ THEN _____

Take care

Always use computers safely and responsibly.

✓ Handle computers and other electronic devices carefully. They can be damaged if dropped.

✓ Protect electronic devices from dust, dirt, and **moisture.**

✓ Electric current can be dangerous. Tell an adult if you see damaged device cables or exposed wires.

✓ Do not share private information such as your phone number, address, or passwords.

✓ Talk to your family about rules for Internet use.

✓ Limit the time you spend on electronic devices. Take frequent breaks to exercise or stretch.

In the space provided, create a poster advertising computer safety tips.

Read the following statements and circle the best response.

You see a damaged power cable on a printer.

- Tell an adult
- Remove the cable and try to repair it

Someone you don't know wants to trade photos online.

- Send photos
- Ignore the request

Your homework requires more online reading than usual.

- Take breaks
- Do the entire assignment all at once

Careers in Computing

Medical professionals often use computer programs that are made especially for their work. For example, many veterinarians use special veterinary programs that store animals' health records and appointment schedules. These custom systems are designed by software developers.

Software developers plan, create, and test computer programs. They consider the needs of users and collect feedback to improve their programs. Software developers must have good communication and problem-solving skills.

Interactive Glossary

As you learn about each term, add notes, drawings, or sentences in the extra space. This will help you remember what the terms mean.
Here are some examples.

fungi [FUHN•jee] A group of organisms that get nutrients by decomposing other organisms

A mushroom is an example of fungi.

physical change [FIHZ•ih•kuhl CHAYNJ] Change in the size, shape, or state of matter with no new substance being formed

When I cut paper in half, that's a physical change.

Glossary Pronunciation Key

With every glossary term, there is also a phonetic respelling.
A phonetic respelling writes the word the way it sounds, which can help you pronounce new or unfamiliar words.
Use this key to help you understand the respellings.

Sound	As in	Phonetic Respelling	Sound	As in	Phonetic Respelling
a	bat	(BAT)	oh	over	(OH•ver)
ah	lock	(LAHK)	oo	pool	(POOL)
air	rare	(RAIR)	ow	out	(OWT)
ar	argue	(AR•gyoo)	oy	foil	(FOYL)
aw	law	(LAW)	s	cell	(SEL)
ay	face	(FAYS)		sit	(SIT)
ch	chapel	(CHAP•uhl)	sh	sheep	(SHEEP)
e	test	(TEST)	th	that	(THAT)
	metric	(MEH•trik)		thin	(THIN)
ee	eat	(EET)	u	pull	(PUL)
	feet	(FEET)	uh	medal	(MED•uhl)
	ski	(SKEE)		talent	(TAL•uhnt)
er	paper	(PAY•per)		pencil	(PEN•suhl)
	fern	(FERN)		onion	(UHN•yuhn)
eye	idea	(eye•DEE•uh)		playful	(PLAY•fuhl)
i	bit	(BIT)		dull	(DUHL)
ing	going	(GOH•ing)	y	yes	(YES)
k	card	(KARD)		ripe	(RYP)
	kite	(KYT)	z	bags	(BAGZ)
ngk	bank	(BANGK)	zh	treasure	(TREZH•er)

A

absorb [ab•SAWRB] **Take in by an object** (p. 250)

amphibian [am•FIB•ee•uhn] **A type of vertebrate that has moist skin, begins its life in water with gills, and develops lungs as an adult to live on land** (p. 304)

arthropod [AHR•thruh•pod] **Animals with jointed legs and hard outer body coverings that make up the largest group of invertebrates** (p. 314)

B

bar graph [BAHR GRAF] **A graph using parallel bars of varying lengths to show comparison** (p. 41)

C

condensation [kahn•duhn•SAY•shuhn] **The process by which water vapor changes into liquid water** (p. 167)

cone [KOHN] **A part of some nonflowering plants where seeds form** (p. 257)

consumer [kuhn•SOOM•er] **A living thing that gets its energy by eating other living things** (p. 354)

D

data [DEY•tuh] **Individual facts, statistics, and items of information** (p. 39)

data table [DEY•tuh TEY•buhl] A set of rows and columns used to record data from investigations (p. 41)

environment [en•VY•ruhn•muhnt] The things, both living and nonliving, that surround a living thing (p. 268)

design process [dih•ZYN PROS•es] The process of applying basic principles of engineering to solve problems (p. 58)

evaporation [ee•vap•uh•RAY•shuhn] The process by which liquid water changes into water vapor (p. 166)

E

electrical energy [ee•LEK•trih•kuhl EN•er•jee] A form of energy that can move through wires (p. 106)

evidence [EV•uh•duhns] Information, collected during an investigation, to support a hypothesis (p. 38)

energy [EN•er•jee] The ability to make something move or change (p. 188)

experiment [ek•SPAIR•uh•muhnt] A test done to see if a hypothesis is correct or not (p. 11)

flower [FLOW•er] **The part of a flowering plant that enables it to reproduce** (p. 256)

gas [GAS] **A form of matter that has no definite shape or volume** (p. 160)

flowering plant [FLOW•er•ing PLANT] **A plant that produces seeds within a fruit** (p. 269)

germinate [JER•muh•nayt] **To start to grow (a seed)** (p. 271)

food chain [FOOD CHAYN] **The flow of food energy in a sequence of living things** (p. 354)

germination [jer•muh•NAY•shuhn] **The sprouting of a seed** (p. 271)

force [FAWRS] **A push or a pull** (p. 120)

graduated cylinder [GRAJ•oo•ay•tid SIL•in•der] **A container marked with a graded scale used for measuring liquids** (p. 23)

© Houghton Mifflin Harcourt Publishing Company

gravity [GRAV•ih•tee] A force that pulls two objects toward each other (p. 120)

infer [in•FER] To draw a conclusion about something (p. 6)

H

heat [HEET] Energy that moves from warmer to cooler objects (p. 226)

insect [IN•sekt] A type of animal that has three body parts and six legs (p. 314)

hibernate [HY•ber•nayt] To go into a deep, sleeplike state for winter (p. 340)

invertebrate [in•VER•tuh•brit] An animal without a backbone (p. 312)

hypothesis [hy•PAHTH•uh•sis] A possible answer to a question that can be tested to see if it is correct (p. 10)

investigation [in•ves•tuh•GAY•shuhn] A study that a scientist does (p. 5)

K

kinetic energy [kih•NET•ik EN•er•jee] **The energy of motion** (p. 188)

matter [MAT•er] **Anything that takes up space** (p. 139)

L

liquid [LIK•wid] **A form of matter that has a volume that stays the same but has a shape that can change** (p. 160)

mechanical energy [muh•KAN•ih•kuhl EN•er•jee] **The total potential and kinetic energy of an object** (p. 188)

M

mammal [MAM•uhl] **A type of vertebrate that has hair or fur and feeds its young with milk from the mother** (p. 307)

microscope [MY•kruh•skohp] **A tool that makes an object look several times bigger than it is** (p. 21)

mass [MAS] **The amount of matter in an object** (p. 23)

migrate [MY•grayt] **To travel from one place to another and back again** (p. 334)

N

nonflowering plant
[non•FLOW•er•ing PLANT] **Plants that reproduce without making flowers** (p. 294)

physical property [FIZ•ih•kuhl PRAHP•er•tee] **Anything that you can observe about an object by using one or more of your senses** (p. 139)

nutrient [NOO•tree•uhnt] **A material in the soil that helps plants grow and stay healthy** (p. 250)

potential energy [poh•TEN•shuhl EN•er•jee] **Energy of position or condition** (p. 188)

O

observe [uhb•ZURV] **To use your senses to gather information** (p. 6)

predict [pri•DIKT] **Use observations and data to form an idea of what will happen under certain conditions** (p. 8)

P

photosynthesis [foht•oh•SIN•thuh•sis] **The process that plants use to make food** (p. 352)

producer [pruh•DOOS•er] **A living thing that makes its own food** (p. 352)

R

reflect [rih•FLEKT] **To bounce off** (p. 206)

refract [rih•FRAKT] **To bend light as it moves from one material to another** (p. 208)

reproduce [ree•pruh•DOOS] **To make more living things of the same kind** (p. 256)

reptile [REP•tyl] **A type of vertebrate that has dry skin covered with scales** (p. 304)

S

seed [SEED] **A structure that contains a young plant and its food supply, surrounded by a protective coat** (p. 256)

shadow [SHAD•oh] **A dark area that forms when an object blocks the path of light** (p. 205)

solid [SAHL•id] **A form of matter that has a volume and a shape that both stay the same** (p. 160)

spore [SPAWR] **A reproductive structure made by some plants, including mosses and ferns, that can grow into a new plant** (p. 296)

star [STAR] **A hot ball of glowing gases that gives off energy** (p. 99)

temperature [TEM•per•uh•cher] **A measure of how hot or cold something is** (p. 144)

sun [SUHN] **The star closest to Earth** (p. 98)

variable [VAIR•ee•uh•buhl] **The one thing that changes in an experiment** (p. 11)

technology [tek•NOL•uh•jee] **Anything that people make or do that changes the natural world** (p. 74)

vertebrate [VER•tuh•brit] **An animal with a backbone** (p. 302)

telescope [TEL•uh•skohp] **A device people use to observe distant objects with their eyes** (p. 104)

volume [VAHL•yoom] **The amount of space that matter takes up** (p. 23)

Index

natural resources
bicycle manufacture and, 178
car manufacture and, 177

nature scientists, 349

Nice, Margaret Morse, 349

non-dash flowering plants, 294
with cones, 294, 298–299
ferns, 296–297
mosses, 296, 299
pine trees, 294
with spores, 296, 298

nutrients, 250–258

observations, 6–7
Ochoa, Ellen, 117–118
orange tree, responding to cold, 272–273
ornithologist, 349
Ortiz, Rosa, 261

pan balance, 22, 141
peach tree, life cycle of, 260
people in science
Burbank, Luther, 349
Chandrasekhar, Subrahmanyan, 117–118
Franklin, Benjamin, 201–202

Liburd, Oscar, 321–322
Nice, Margaret Morse, 349
Ochoa, Ellen, 117–118
Ortiz, Rosa, 261
Turner, Charles, 321–322

photosynthesis, 352–359
needs for, 360
plants produce, 353
plants take in, 353

physical properties, 139–145

pine needles, 291

pine trees, 294. *See also* **cones**

plants. *See also* **animals**
botanist, 261–262
budding, 271, 277
classifying, 290–291, 325–326
cone, 257
draw conclusions, 266, 326, 348
in environment, 267–277
in fall, 338, 342
food, 254
and gravity, 274, 275
and heat, 270–271
kinds of, 290, 298
leaves, 259
life cycle, seed-bearing, 256–257
and light, 265–266 268–269, 276
maple leaves, 291
needs of, 347–348
palm leaves, 291

parts, 291
pine needles, 291
record data, 265, 325, 348
reproduce, 258
seed, 256, 258
in spring, 335, 342
in summer, 336, 342
sundew, 289
sun energy of, 352
water and nutrients for, 254
in winter, 272–273, 236, 242

potential energy, 188–189, 194–195. *See also* **energy**

Ponce de Leon Inlet Lighthouse, 55

predictions, 8

producer, 352, 358–360
corn, 356

prototypes, 262–263

pull, 120–121, 125, 274. *See also* **gravity**

push, 120, 125

radiant energy, 102–103, 107. *See also* **energy**

reading skills
cause and effect, 119, 203, 209, 254, 338
clue words, 226
compare and contrast, 99, 137, 251
draw conclusions, 112, 116, 154, 158, 174, 218, 240, 266, 326, 348

main idea and details,
37, 42, 124, 187,
225, 252, 267, 276,
311, 334, 336, 351
sequence, 249, 351
signal words, 73, 159,
203, 301
using headings, 97
visual aids, 289, 333
record data, 37–41, 43,
47, 72, 87, 111, 115, 153,
157, 173, 217, 239, 265,
325, 348
bar graph, 41, 43
communicating data,
40–41
data table, 41, 43
evidence, 38–39,
43–44
record your results, 17, 33
rectangular solid, 142
red stars, 101
reflections, 207–208,
210–212, 214–218
refraction, 208–212, 214
reproduce, 256, 258
reptiles, 304, 308
alligator, 305
boa, 302
characteristics of,
304–305
frilled lizard, 305
gecko, 305
loggerhead turtle, 333,
337, 339
rattlesnake, 355
snake, 309, 336
turtle, 304, 308
robins in summer, 336
rocket, opposing gravity,
122, 126

roots, 259
carrot, 251
compare and contrast,
251
functions, 250
grass, 251
growth responding to
gravity, 274–276, 277
of moonseed, 261
pansy, 251

S

science, 4–11. *See also*
inquiry skills
drawing conclusions, 1
experiments and
variables, 10–11
hypothesis, 10–11
investigations, 5, 9–11
models and maps, 9
observations and
interferences, 6–7
predictions, 8
records, 27
tools, 20–25, 27
scientists. *See also*
**Careers in Science;
People in Science**
communicate, 39–41
nature, 349
record data, 37
seasons, 333–341
sea turtles, South Florida, 1
seedling, 256–257, 260
seeds, 256, 258, 293
germinate, 271
set a purpose, 16, 17, 32,
33, 46, 47, 70, 71, 86,
87, 110, 114, 152, 156,
172, 216, 238, 263,
324, 346

sequence, 249–351
sequoia, 294–295.
See also **cones**
shadow, 205, 212
signal words, 73, 159,
203, 301
size, 139
sky walk, 123
snake in summer, 336
solids, 160
sound, 190, 192–193,
195–196.
See also **energy spores,**
296, 299
moss and fern, 297
**South Florida Symphony
spoonbill, Roseate,** 287
spring
animals in, 334,
341–342
germination in,
334, 343
plants in, 335, 342
star, 99, 106–107.
See also **sun**
brightness, 101, 106
color, 101, 106–107
compare and contrast
with sun, 99
draw conclusions, 112
number of, 111–112
record data, 111
size, 101, 106
star gazers, 117, 118
star gazing, 104, 108
state your hypothesis, 17,
47, 71
stem, 259
bamboo, 253
broccoli, 253
dogwood, 253